70 IDEAS FROM GLOBAL BEST INTERIOR DESIGN II

ARTPOWER

70 Ideas From Global Best Interior Design II

© Artpower International Publishing Co., Ltd. – ACS

ACS | ARTPOWER

Publisher: Lu Jican
Chief Editor: Li Aihong, Wang Chen
Executive Editor: Zhou Ziqing, Xu Kexin, You Tong
Art Designer: Chen Ting, Xiong Libo

Registered Address
Flat B5 1/F, Manning Ind.Bldg., 116-118 How Ming St., Kwun Tong, Kowloon, Hong Kong, China
Tel: 852-23977886
Fax: 852-23982111

Editorial Department
Address: 5021-5023, 5th Floor, Phase II of Art Design Center, Zhanyi Road, Luohu District, Shenzhen, China
Tel: 86-755-25111140
Fax: 86-755-82020029

Web: www.artpower.com.cn / www.acs.cn
Sales & Distribution: overseasales@artpower.com.cn
Press & Editorial Submissions: press@artpower.com.cn / contact@artpower.com.cn

ISBN 978-988-14688-7-1

All Rights Reserved. No part of this publication may be reproduced or utilised in any form by any means, electronic or mechanical, including photocopying, recording or by any information storage and retrieval system, without prior written permission of the publisher.

All images in this book have been reproduced with the knowledge and prior consent of the designers and the clients concerned, and every effort has been made to ensure that credits accurately comply with information applied. No responsibility is accepted by producer, publisher, or printer for any infringement of copyright or otherwise arising from the contents of this publication.

Printed and bound in China.

PREFACE

"Global Best Interior" is a beautiful compilation of a hand-picked selection of interior architecture and design projects from around the world. With an attention to the overall character of a space, down to the details that breathe life into the skin of a building or space, it provides its reader with an enjoyable insight into each project.

The Can Bordoy Grand House & Garden Hotel from OHLAB is a perfect example of the power that good interior design can have. The seemingly effortless combination of the old and the new, merge in a harmonious symphony of functions, shades, materials, and forms. Each part of the building, from the floors to the walls and ceilings, the ensemble of furniture, fabrics, and art – all complement each other, without hoarding the focus to any one aspect. The ambiance created, makes one feel blissfully comfortable with a noble note. Nothing feels forced – just the way it should be.

The residential space Modern Zen from ZRIVERSTUDIO is another beautiful interior, where simplicity leaves space for one to fully appreciate each surface and object. Its minimal style, combined flamboyant pieces, speaks a clear language and provides enough space for the eyes to breathe and absorb the unique details staged throughout the space.

Interior architecture and design trends are taking us into exciting new dimensions. Organic shapes and softer forms are taking the place of hard, sharp edges. While still holding true to the need for comfort and beauty, we will find a growth in interiors with spaces for the eyes to breathe and love for the details. Forms that invite one's gaze to caress their curves and shades or contrasting shapes and surfaces to provide the necessary freshness.

We will not only see the continuation of the trend to bring the outdoors in, as the need to connect with nature is recognized as a key element to maintaining a balance to the busy lives we live, with most time spent indoors, but we will also see the indoors being moved out. The division between the in and out will continue to fade.

Joanna Lehnis
noa* network of architecture

CONTENTS

PUBLIC SPACE

- 008 Fuzhou Strait Culture And Art Centre
- 022 Tianjin Binhai Library
- 028 Harbin Opera House
- 040 Thailand Creative And Design Centre (TCDC)
- 052 Helsinki Central Library Oodi

HOTEL SPACE

- 064 Gloriette Guesthouse
- 074 La Suite Hotel
- 084 Hotel Ease
- 094 Can Bordoy Grand House & Garden
- 104 Cretan Malia Park

RESIDENTIAL SPACE

- 120 Albert Court Apartment
- 128 Kennedy Residence
- 134 Show Apartment "Shades Of Grey"
- 140 Serenity In The City
- 146 Modern Zen

OFFICE SPACE

- 156 Artek Headquarter Helsinki
- 164 Underwater Office
- 170 Tencent Seafront Towers
- 178 Sivantos Singapore

COMMERCIAL SPACE

- 186 Open House
- 194 Molecure Pharmacy
- 202 Cor Shop
- 210 Galeries Lafayette Flagship On Champs-Élysées
- 218 Shiseido
- 226 Delvaux "le 27" In Brussels

FOOD SPACE

- 236 Fish On Fire
- 242 Gaga King Glory
- 250 Cocina Hermanos Torres Restaurant
- 258 Sintoho Restaurant At The Four Seasons Hotel
- 268 Wood Mountain—Anti-domino No. 02

EXHIBITION SPACE

- 280 The Culinary Village: Arda Showroom
- 288 Grupo Arca, Design Center Guadalajara

1

PUBLIC SPACE

Public Space

Fuzhou Strait Culture And Art Centre

Design Agency
PES-Architects

Local Partner
China Construction Engineering Design Group Corporation Ltd.

Area
153,000 m²

Photography
Marc Goodwin, Zhang Yong

The Fuzhou Strait Culture and Art Centre is designed by PES-Architects, and it is their seventh project in China. The project is located in Fuzhou, the capital of Fujian Province, which is one of the largest cities in the province. It has been ranked one of the fastest growing metropolitan areas in the world. The Fuzhou Government hosted an international invited competition for this project with the goal of strengthening the cultural image of the city and the Mawei New Town development area.

Take Inspiration from the Plant

PES-Architects' winning proposal takes inspiration from the petals of a jasmine blossom, the city flower of Fuzhou. The five jasmine petal venues are opera house (1,600 seats), concert hall (1,000 seats), multi-functional theatre, art exhibition hall and cinema centre, which are linked by a cultural concourse and a large roof terrace.

The roof terrace is accessible via two ramps from the Jasmine Gardens as well as from the Central Jasmine Plaza, providing a seamless connection from the complex to the riverfront of the Minjiang River. On the underground level, a promenade-like route along the Liangcuo River connects the landscape to the interiors, as well as providing a connection between the metro station and the centre.

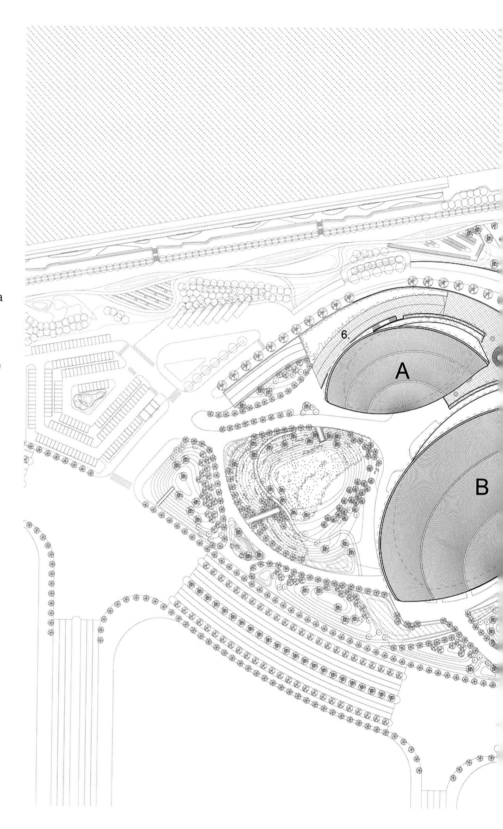

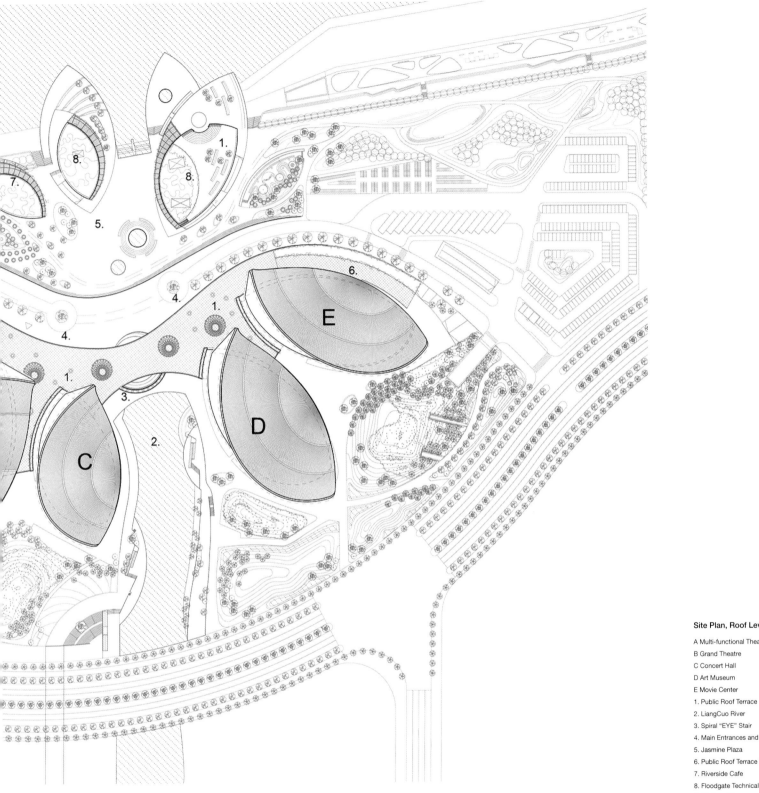

Site Plan, Roof Level

A Multi-functional Theatre
B Grand Theatre
C Concert Hall
D Art Museum
E Movie Center
1. Public Roof Terrace
2. LiangCuo River
3. Spiral "EYE" Stair
4. Main Entrances and Drop-off
5. Jasmine Plaza
6. Public Roof Terrace Ramps
7. Riverside Cafe
8. Floodgate Technical Spaces
9. Minjiang River

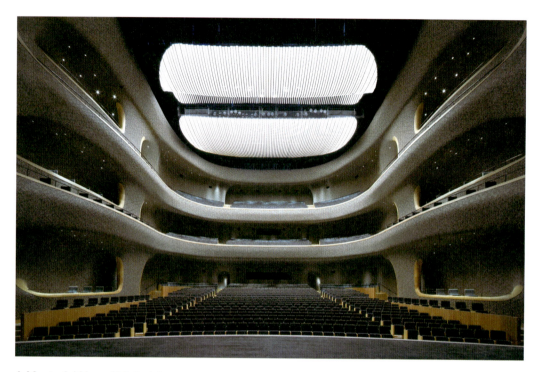

A Masterful Use of Materials

Ceramics, a traditional material with a cultural heritage, is used as the project's main material due to its significance in the historical context of the maritime Silk Road trade connection between China and the rest of the world. PES-Architects worked with Taiwanese ceramic artist Samuel Hsuan-yu Shih to design the artistic ceramic interior for two main auditoriums according to acoustical demands, using the legendary "China White" material and new technology. All facades are clad with white ceramic tiles.

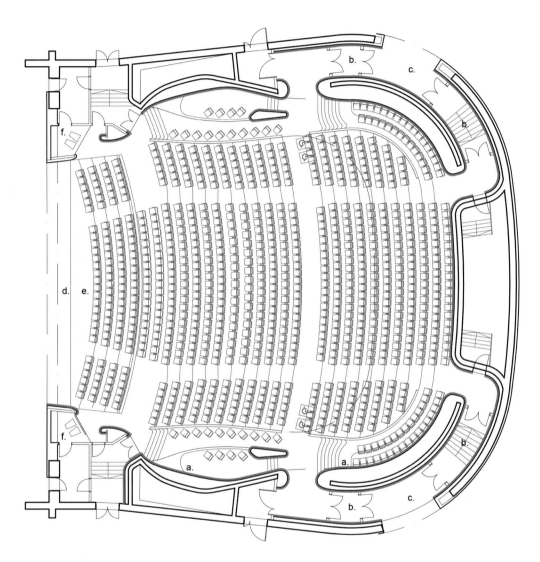

Opera Auditorium Plan, Main Stalls

a. Ceramic Tiles Covering Double Curved GRG Panels
b. Sound Lock Room
c. Audience Entrances
d. Stage
e. Orchestra Pit Lift / Temporary Seating
f. Proscenium with Integrated Speaker and Lighting

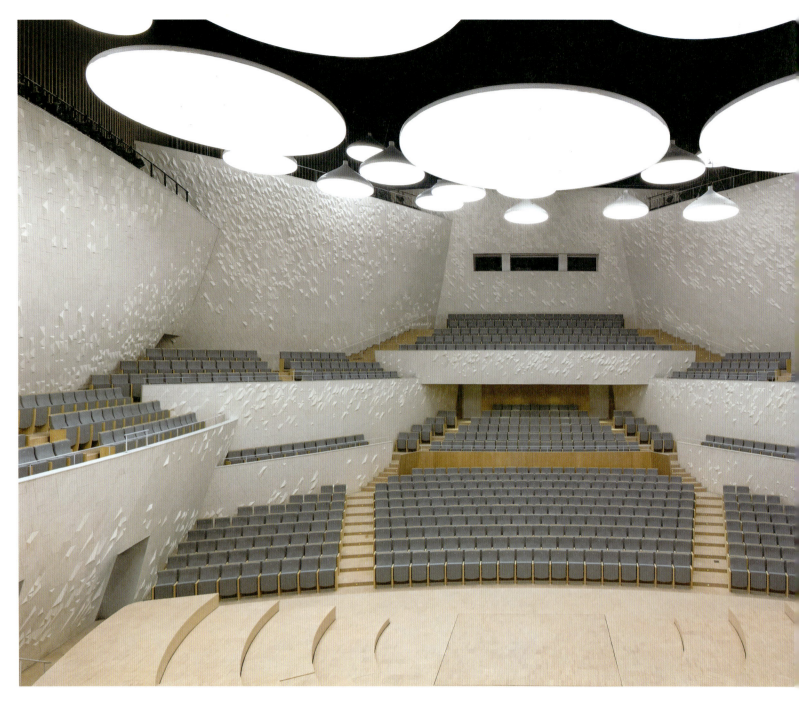

The interior surfaces of the opera hall and concert hall are clad with topographical ceramic panels. Based on extensive studies carried out with the acousticians, two types of acoustic panels are developed: an engraved panel and a mosaic tile panel. Both panels are adaptable to the topographical surfaces that are required to achieve high quality acoustics, as well as the visual language of the design.

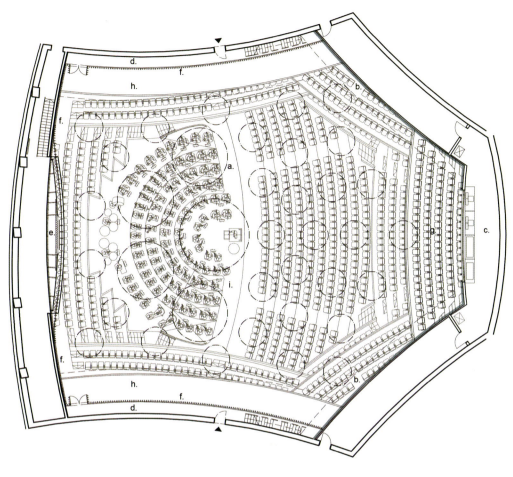

Concert Hall Auditorium Plan

a. Suspended Acoustic Reflector / "Light Cloud"
b. China white Tiles on GRG Surface
c. Sound and Light Control Room
d. Acoustic Curtain Space
e. Organ
f. Vertical
g. Real Balcony
h. Technical Balcony
i. Stage

The Multipurpose Hall is designed for a 700-seat audience. The walls are clad with solid CNC cut bamboo blocks, shaped according to the acoustic needs. The roof is equipped with a flexible cable net ceiling to enable a flexible usage of lighting and other technical equipment.

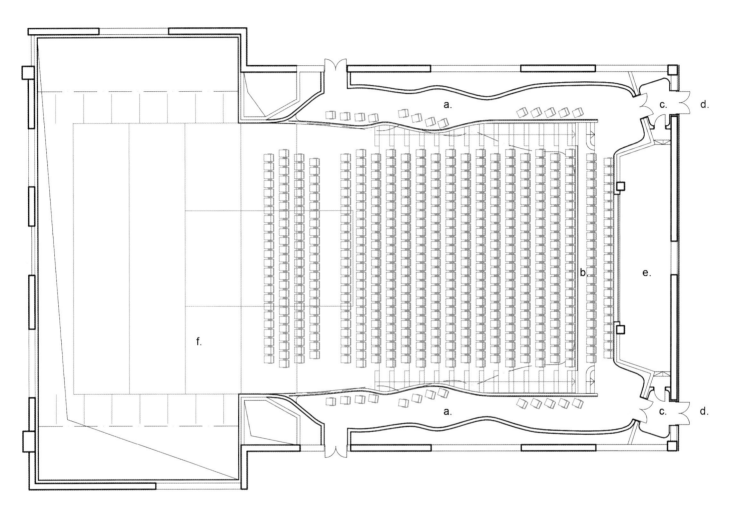

Multifunctional Hall Auditorium Plan, 1st Balcony

a. Side Balconies
b. 1st Balcony
c. Sound Lock
d. Audience Entrance
e. Sound and Light Control
f. Stage

Public Space

Tianjin Binhai Library

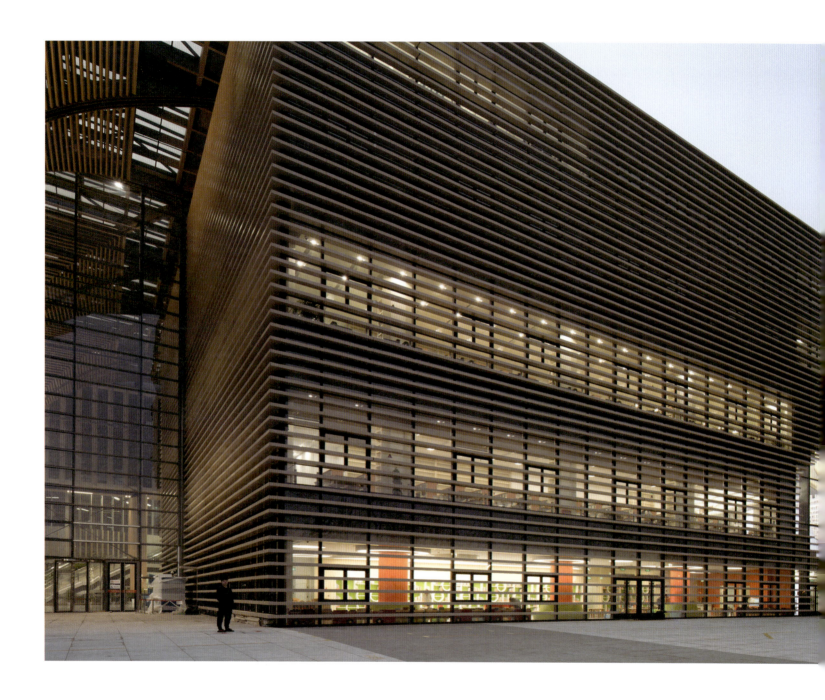

Design Agency
MVRDV

Location
Tianjin, China

Area
33,700 m²

Photography
Ossip van Duivenbode

MVRDV in collaboration with local architects TUPDI has completed the Tianjin Binhai Library, which is one of a cluster of five cultural buildings. It is intended to be the "The Eye" and the "Sea of Knowledge". The library has gone viral for its very technological look.

The Binhai Library has a floor area of 33,700 m^2, with 22,580 m^2 on five floors above ground and 8,120 m^2 on the ground floor and is designed for a total collection of 1.2 million books, 1,200 seats for readers, and a daily capacity of 4,000 readers.

Creating a Visual Point in the Centre of a Space

A spherical auditorium with a diameter of 21m occupies the central position and contrasts sharply with the flat exterior of the building. The exterior of the spherical auditorium is covered with luminous equipment and the interior is a multi-purpose hall with a capacity of more than 100 people. Facing the sphere is an oval opening that looks like a giant eye looking out from the outside. The indoor space and the view of the park outside the pavilion are reflected in the mirror, creating a rich spatial hierarchy.

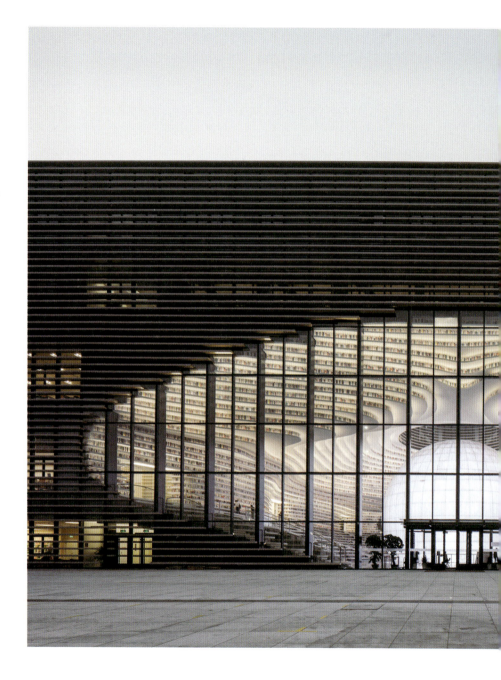

Another highlight is the "book mountain" shaped ladder in the cave-like interior. The white steps are laid out in a wavy pattern, allowing readers to pick up books from the continuously wavy shelves. The corrugated steps taper at the top to form a domed space like a church vault, running up and down, linking all levels and echoing the spherical auditorium in the atrium.

The unique layout shapes numerous spaces for resting, reading, relaxing, climbing and paths to everywhere. MVRDV co-founder Winy Maas says: "The mirrored sphere at the heart of the building is the core of the library, a window to a 360-degree panorama, and a space that really prompts one to think."

Rational Planning of Each Floor

The five-level building also contains extensive educational facilities, arrayed along the edges of the interior and accessible through the main atrium space. Public program is supported by subterranean service spaces, book storage, and a large archive. From the ground floor visitors can easily access reading areas for children and the elderly, the auditorium, the main entrance, terraced access to the floors above and connection to the cultural complex. The first and second floors consist primarily of reading rooms, books and lounge areas whilst the upper floors also include meeting rooms, offices, computer and audio rooms and two roof top patios.

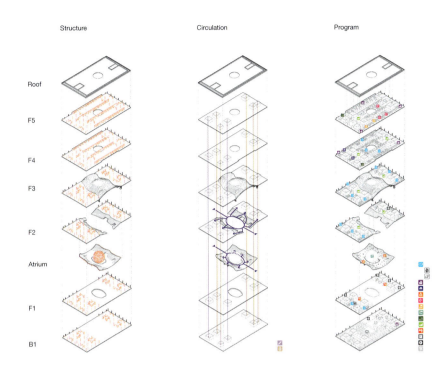

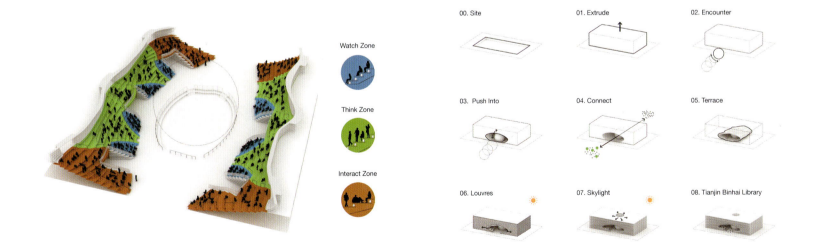

Public Space

Harbin Opera House

Architects
MAD Architect

Location
Heilongjiang, China

Photography
Hufton+Crow, Adam Mørk

Situated on the northern bank of the Songhua River, the Harbin Opera Theatre is a public cultural building set in the natural landscape of the North, inspired by the natural landscape of the surrounding wetlands and the frozen character of the North. Designed by MAD Architects under the direction of Ma Yansong, the 1.8 km² site has a gross floor area of 79,000 m² and comprises a 1,600-seat theatre and a 400-seat small theatre.

The white skin of the theatre seems to be a breathing cell, "photosynthesising" under the northern sun. The building is like a floating ribbon, breaking out of the wetlands, growing out of nature and becoming part of the white horizon of the North. In contrast to the city skyline south of the Songhua River, the beauty and uniqueness of nature is present here, making the Harbin Opera Theatre a functional, but at the same time, an earthy landscape where humanity, art and nature merge.

Deepen the Emotional Connection of the Public with the Environment

Unlike typical landmarks, the Harbin Opera House does not stand in isolation in the city, but is an "intimate" building accessible from all sides, with an emphasis on citizen interaction and participation. The amphitheatre and viewing platform at the top of the building is open to the public, becoming a vertical extension of the park, offering views of the city skyline and surrounding natural landscape to the south and north of the Songhua River. Even if they do not enter the theatre to watch a performance, the public can walk from the surrounding park and square to the roof through the ramp that wraps around the exterior of the building, getting up close to the building with their bodies and experiencing the theatrical experience and mood.

The musician Comballo once said, "Music is the sound of thinking." The Harbin Opera Theatre provides the right ambient place to produce such sounds and becomes a building that interacts with people and nature from the physical to the spiritual, allowing us to rethink the relationship between people and nature. In addition, the acoustic design of the theatre's interior, which has been tested in practice, has been rated by Chinese, European and American acoustics experts as "a grand theatre of international excellence in acoustic performance".

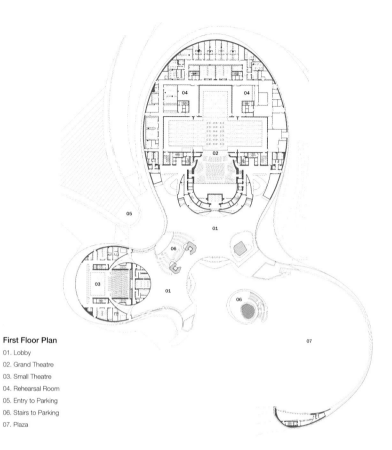

First Floor Plan
01. Lobby
02. Grand Theatre
03. Small Theatre
04. Rehearsal Room
05. Entry to Parking
06. Stairs to Parking
07. Plaza

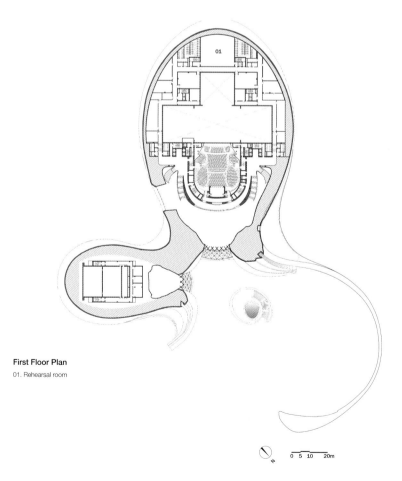

First Floor Plan
01. Rehearsal room

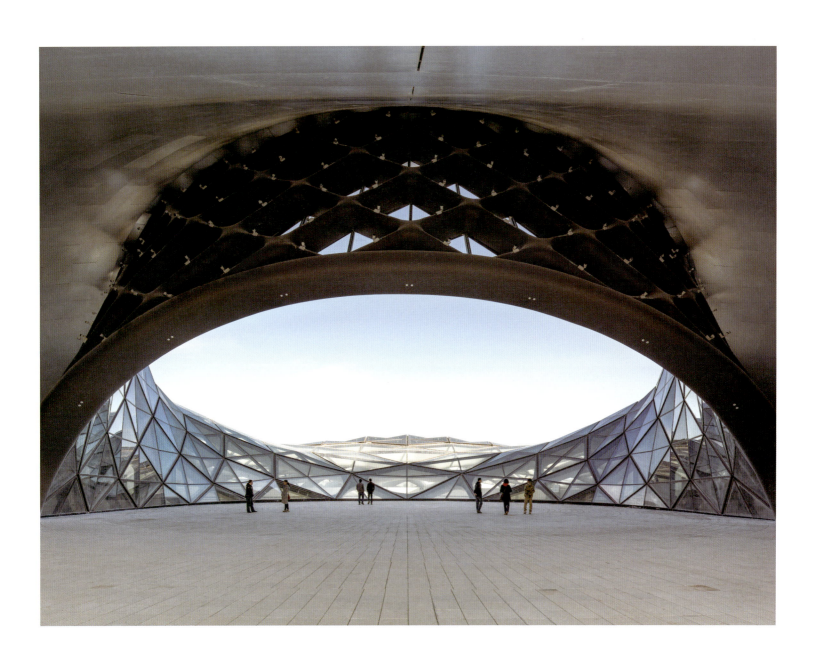

The Interplay of Space and Mind

The glass skylight at the top brings maximum natural light into the room, which spills onto the atrium of the theatre's Manchurian Ash walls, highlighting the combination of the walls and local materials, handcrafted with pure artisanship, so that wherever one goes, one can feel the transparency and ethereality of daylight pouring in.

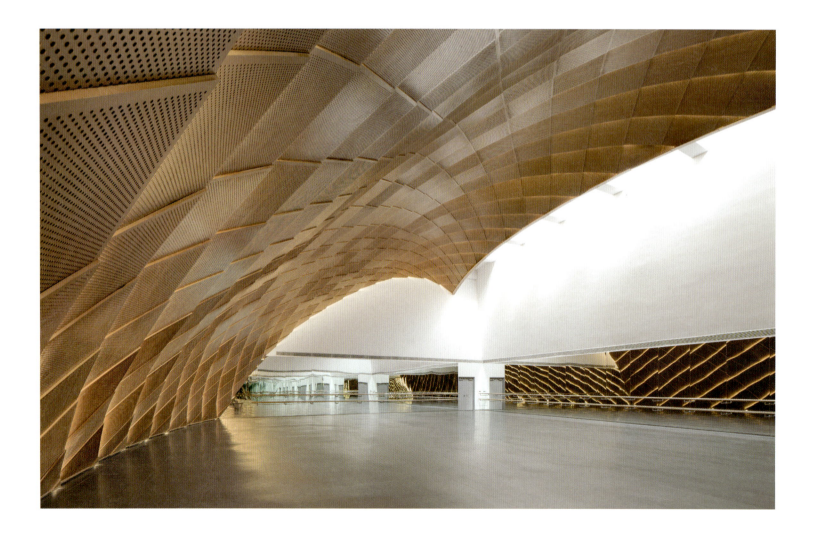

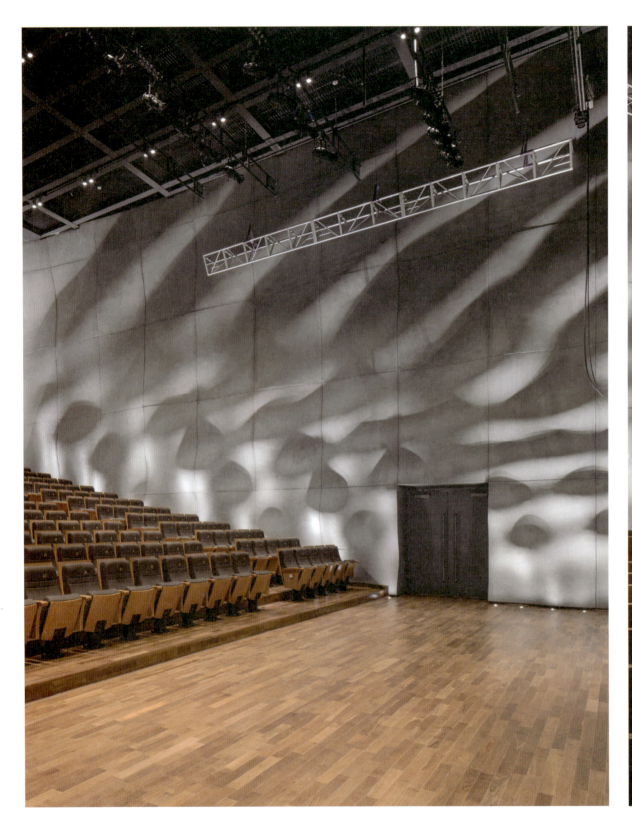

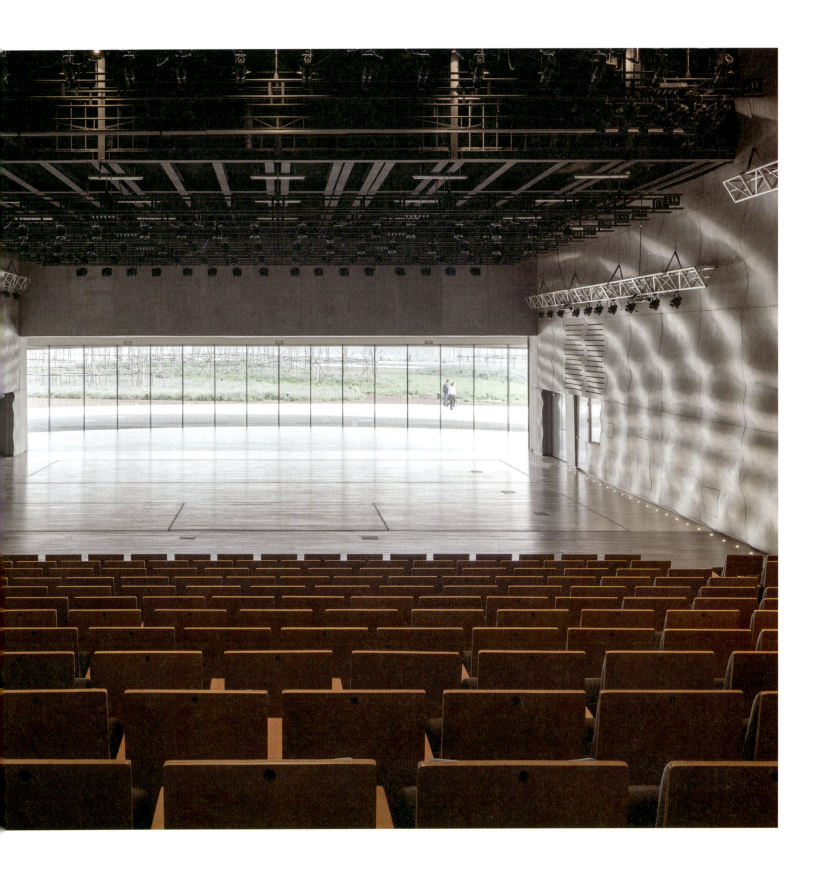

The backstage of the small theatre is also designed with transparent acoustic glass, allowing the natural outdoor environment to become an extension and backdrop to the stage, offering new possibilities for the creation of the stage in the small theatre. The amphitheatre is handcrafted from bent willow, with a soft and warm atmosphere, natural textures and varied organic forms, giving a sense of life to the space. The architectural space resembles an amplified musical instrument, and when you are in it, it is as if you can see the sound flowing through the space.

The simple purity of the materials and the varied spatial combinations provide the conditions for optimum acoustics. The dust in the backlight also seems to be a reminder that this is a hyper-sensitive space in which the audience becomes both the observed and the performer, and that one's consciousness has begun to enter a sort of abstract, detached reality before the play is staged.

Public Space

Thailand Creative
And Design Centre (TCDC)

Design Agency
Department of ARCHITECTURE Co.

Location
Bangkok, Thailand

Area
9,950 m²

Photography
W Workspace

Thailand Creative and Design Centre (Abbreviated TCDC) is a government agency with a mission to inspire creative thinking and propel the country's creative economy. It provides a broad range of resources and services: a design library, a material library, a co-working space, a maker space, exhibitions, lectures, workshops, etc.

TCDC is now moved into a wing of the historical Grand Postal Building. The design of the space is intended for the new intervention to have a dialogue with the old building and at the same time to answer to TCDC's mission to be the country's creative incubator.

The Embodiment of Creativity is not Because How it Looks

A creative space is not "creative" because of how it looks but it is a place that inspires. The free flow open workspace spread throughout the building is designed to encourage informal conversations. The main circulation cut through the section of the building bringing people to flow pass different facilities to be inspired by what others are doing. Exhibition nodes are integrated into all spaces where fresh ideas always surround us.

Within the historical building, the new is inserted as an object, placing within and offsetting from the existing envelope, clearly revealing architectural features from the 30's. The present-day material in its light, translucent, blurring, and glowing quality is having a dialogue with the massive character of the historical shell. The new and the old are interestingly contrasting, enhancing and complementing one another.

This translucent architectural system surrounds and inserts itself throughout the facility and contains the essence of what TCDC has to offer — inspiration and knowledge. It is designed to contain everything from books, magazines, material samples, digital media, mini exhibition, brainstorm boards, communication boards, announcement, etc. The inspiration runs through and encompasses all the creative spaces.

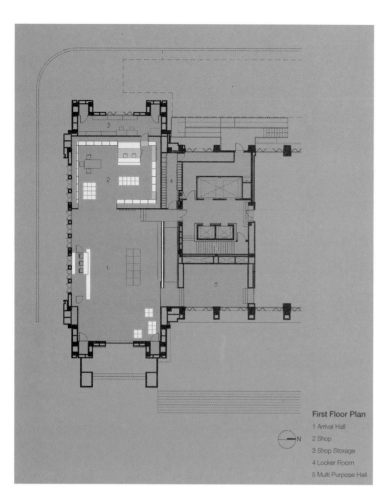

First Floor Plan
1 Arrival Hall
2 Shop
3 Shop Storage
4 Locker Room
5 Multi Purpose Hall

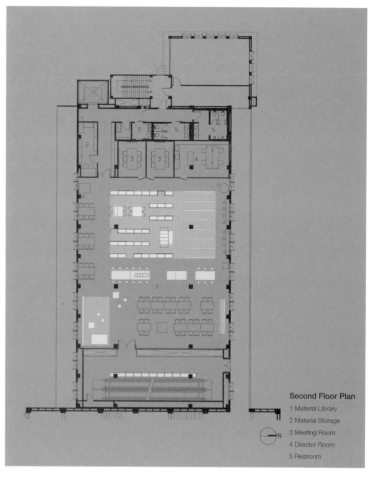

Second Floor Plan
1 Material Library
2 Material Storage
3 Meeting Room
4 Director Room
5 Restroom

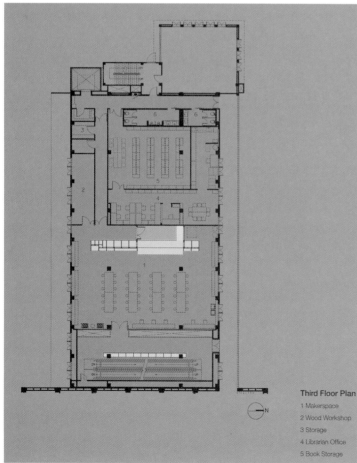

Third Floor Plan
1 Makerspace
2 Wood Workshop
3 Storage
4 Librarian Office
5 Book Storage

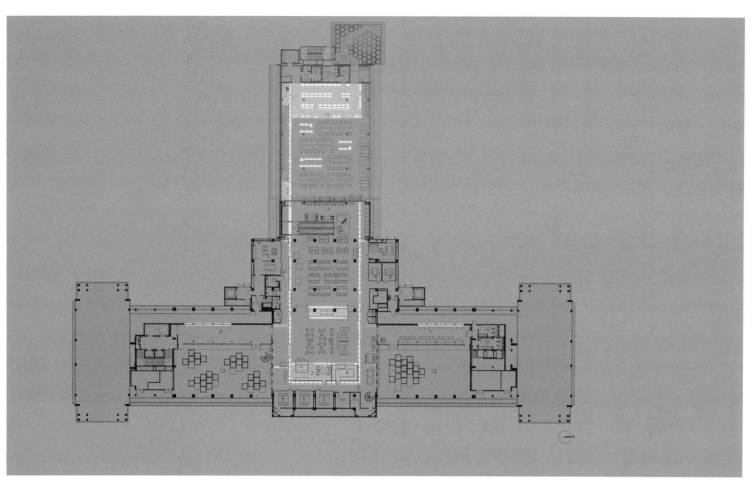

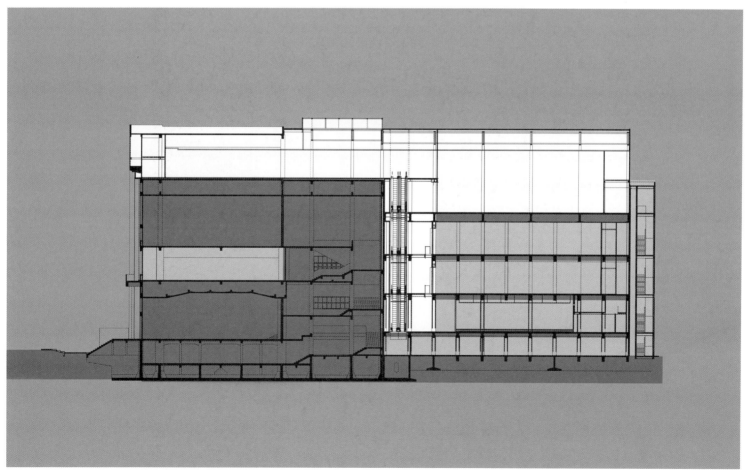

Public Space

Helsinki Central Library Oodi

Design Agency
ALA Architects

Location
Helsinki, Finland

Area
17,100 m²

Photography
Tuomas Uusheimo

Helsinki Central Library Oodi in the heart of Helsinki consists almost entirely of public space and offers a wide selection of services. It is the new central point of the city's impressive public library network and represents a new era of libraries.

Good Design is Site-specific

Oodi has been built using local materials and with local climate conditions in mind. The wooden facade is made from pre-fabricated elements. 33 mm thick Finnish premium spruce was used for the cladding. A specific grading and quality control system was developed for the timber, the sawing and the treatment of the slats. The complex curved geometry was designed and manufactured using algorithm-aided parametric 3D design methods in order to achieve the required precision. The appearance of the facade will develop over the years towards a deeper, richer version of its initial hue.

The carefully planned placement and optimization of building services has enabled the flexibility of the spatial arrangements. All public levels of the building are equipped with access floors to allow for changes in use during the estimated 150-year life span of the building.

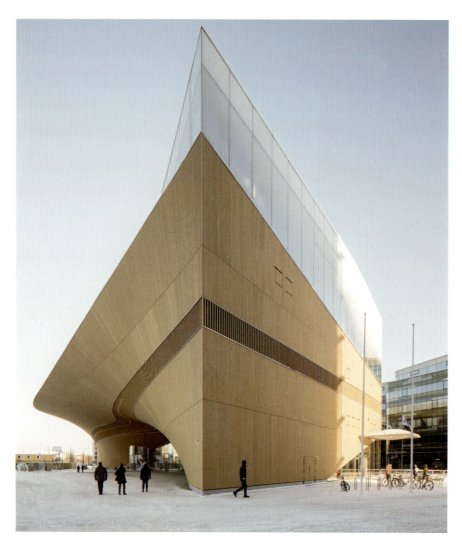

Design for Practicality

The design divides the functions of the library into three distinct levels: an active ground floor, a peaceful upper floor, and an enclosed in-between volume containing the more specific functions.

The library is opening directly to the surrounding cityscape and dissolving the border between indoor and outdoor areas. The large foyer and the glass-walled multi-purpose hall on ground level act as indoor extensions of the outdoor spaces. The Kansalaistori square (Citizens' Square) across the street from the Parliament House seamlessly continues inside the ground floor level of the library building. The arching form invites people to utilize the spaces and services underneath, inside and on top of it. The flexible spaces are suitable for both small events and large happenings. The multi-purpose hall can be used as part of the open lobby space or separated off to cater for specific events.

The building's structural solution is based on asymmetrical bridge spanning over 100 meters over the open ground floor space. The bridge structure consisting of steel trusses and beams is supported by two massive steel arches, tensioned together with a reinforced concrete tension slab.

The innovative structural solution has enabled both the construction of the flexible column-free interior spaces and the possibility for the construction of a future road tunnel under the site. Secondary steel trusses support the cantilevering balcony and roof canopy asymmetrically from the arch structure, forming a unique structural design to accommodate both permanent and temporary functions for both the library and the public realm.

The "Book Heaven" on the top floor, is a vast open landscape topped with an undulating cloud like white ceiling. A calm, serene atmosphere invites visitors to read, learn, think, and enjoy themselves. From this level visitors can enjoy an unobstructed 360-degree panorama view of the city centre.

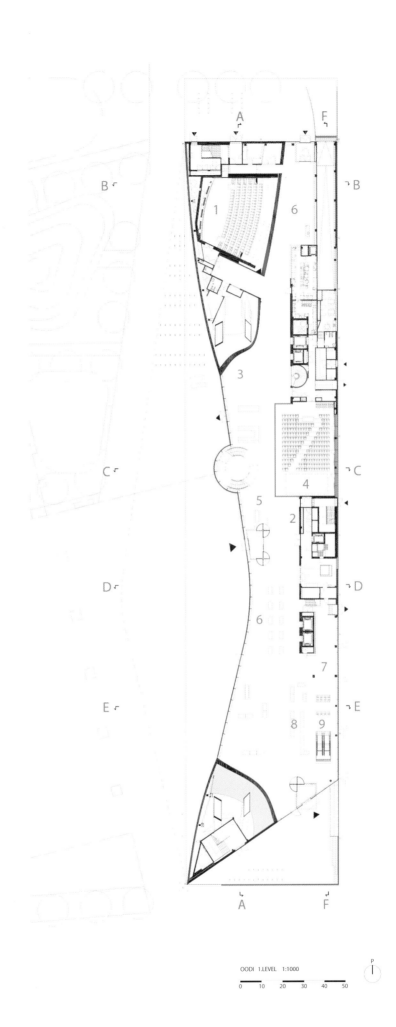

OODI 1.LEVEL 1:1000

0 10 20 30 40 50

1 Cinema
2 Automated Book Return
3 Restaurant
4 Multi-Purpose Hall
5 Foyer
6 Foyer
7 Europa Experience
8 Info
9 Client Computers

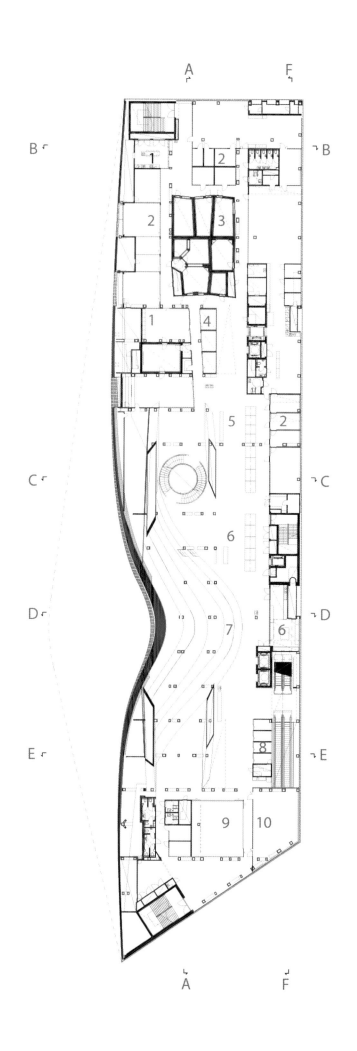

1 Learning Spaces
2 Group Rooms
3 Studios
4 Game Rooms
5 Workstations
6 Urban Workshop
7 Sitting Steps
8 Individual Working Rooms
9 Event Space Kuutio
10 Reading Room

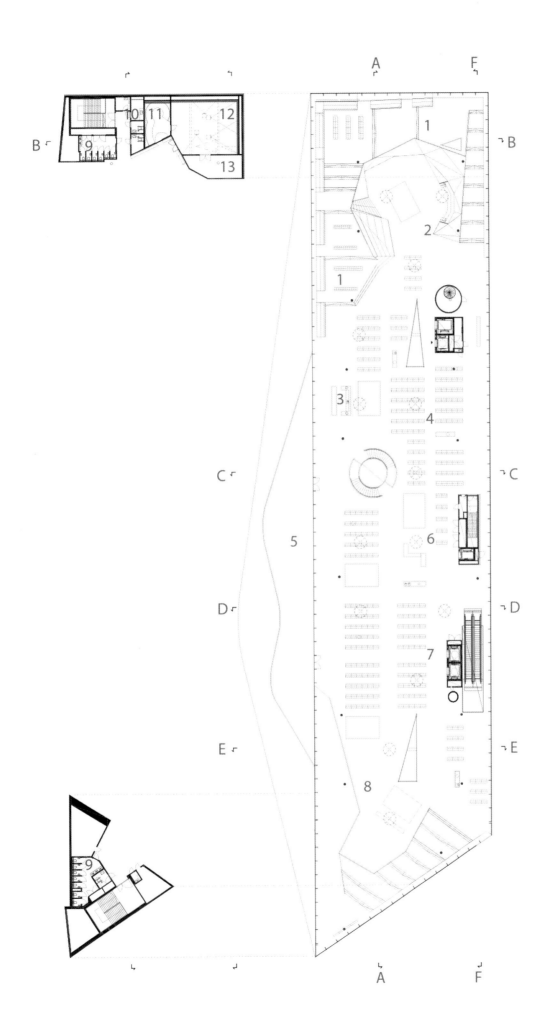

1 Childrens Materials
2 Children and Families
3 Cafe
4 Fiction
5 Balcony
6 Reservations
7 Non-Fiction
8 Newspapers
9 Toliet
10 Nursing Room
11 Fairytale Room
12 Event Space
13 Storage

2

HOTEL SPACE

Hotel Space

Gloriette Guesthouse

Design Agency

noa* (network of architecture)

Location

Renon, Italy

Area

2,000 m²

Photography

Alex Filz

Gloriette Guesthouse by noa* builds at Ritten, a small city in northern Italy. The architectural typology in timelessly, elegant Art Nouveau that seeks simplicity of form without giving up completely on luxury and comfort on the Ritten transposed — generous, classic, simple, but not sober.

Incorporating Local Fashions

The holistic design approach is clearly visible: numerous details form a common thread running through the entire project. It is essential for noa* to incorporate locally prevalent elements, such as the rhombus, the most favoured local element that appears amongst the many railroad-houses along the Ritten railway.

Another element, the "arch", recurs throughout the building in this case. For example, the windows, arched opening allows the quality of the outer spaces to become more visible and tangible, with the frameless windows the room seems to continue as far as the parapet. For example, in the rooms as a mirror that is rounded at the bottom, as a fireplace in the lounge, where the arch is extruded around its own axis, or as the lounger's backrest at the spa terrace.

Creating a Visual Focal Point

In the public area, a seamless resin floor was chosen as an element to allow the room to flow continuously. "Islands" with wooden flooring were created within the floors that define the different areas of the lounge and restaurant. The furniture is mostly freestanding and loosely positioned, elegant and plain upholstery enhance the ambience. Amidst everything are unique finds from flea markets or little treasures from the previous hotel. Dispersed throughout the building are golden lamp sculptures hanging from the ceilings.

Not only in the public area and the spa, but especially in the guestrooms and suites, a passionate focus on the interior is omnipresent. Special attention is paid to the suites' bay windows, which offer lounge areas with a fireplace, free-standing bathtubs or sofa landscapes. Spaces are defined with room-in-room shells, where wall, floor and ceiling are furnished with the same material. The appealing and inviting atmosphere is also achieved through the use of wood, which never appears rustic but noble, homogenously plain, without being cold.

Swimming Pool "Suspended" in the Air

Certainly, the biggest highlight, visible from a distance, is the spa area, which has an extravagant cantilevered swimming pool. The shell, in which the pool is enclosed, is covered with the bronze-coloured aluminium panels. When entering from the rear end, the pool is covered with a bronze-coloured rounded shell, which increasingly dissolves into a rounded net structure of poles, until one swims out under the open sky. This almost sculptural appearing structure of poles is yet another interpretation of the ever appearing arch and the rhombus — closer observation allows one to see that the curved poles create a rhombus when intersecting.

The automatic sliding door opens and one descends into the water, accompanied by the curved shell, one is lead towards the horizon in the infinity pool and enjoy a fascinating play of reflections. It is a process of soft fading out that dissolves this cylindrical shell and thus triggers the feeling of floating while enjoying the distant view. This may well be the summit of a journey that might have been imagined even before entering the building.

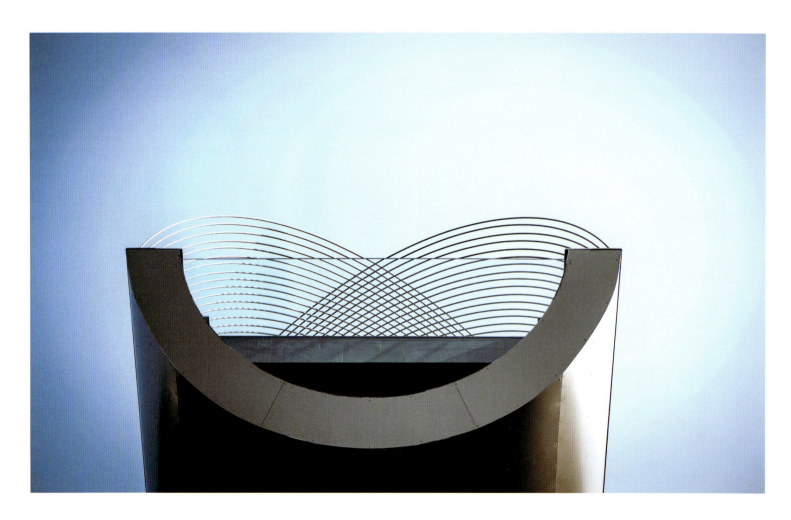

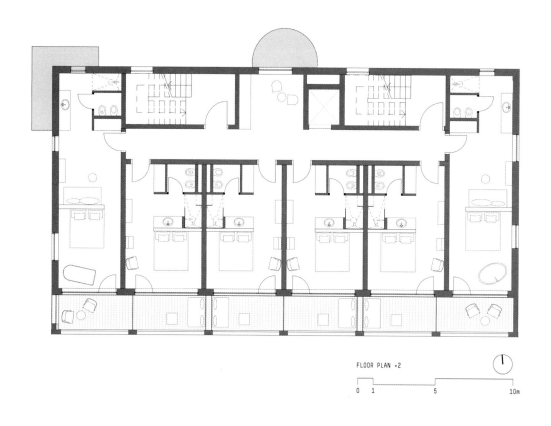

FLOOR PLAN +2

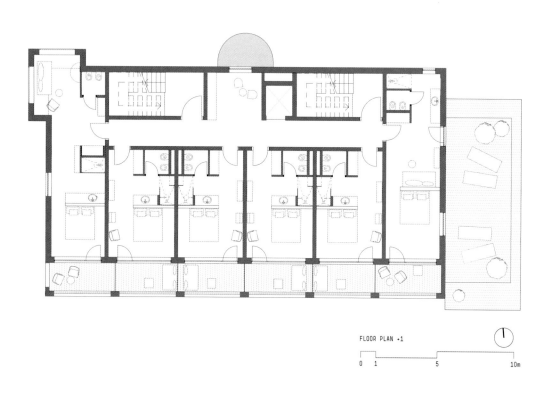

FLOOR PLAN +1

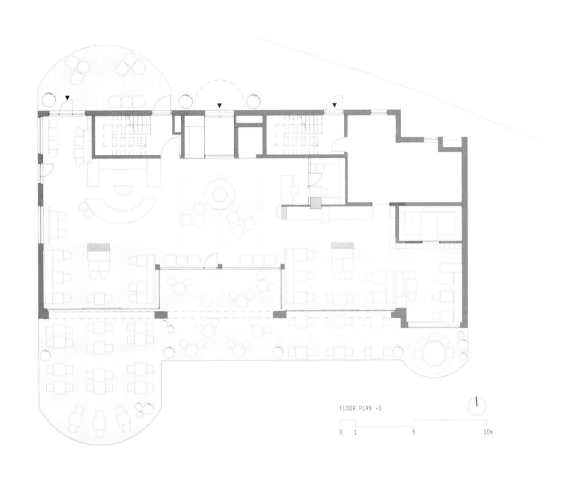

FLOOR PLAN +0

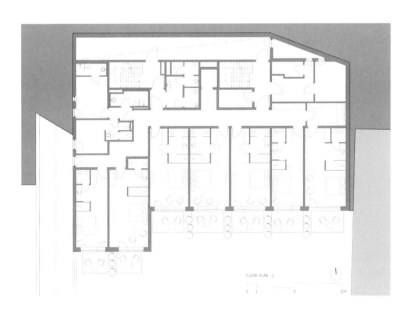

FLOOR PLAN -1

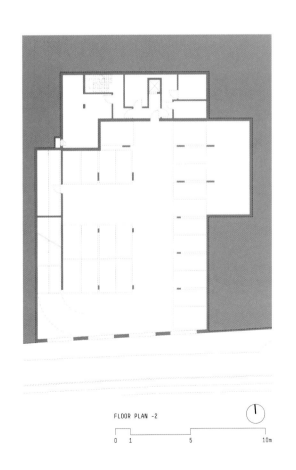

FLOOR PLAN -2

073

Hotel Space

La Suite Hotel

Design Agency
Studio Marco Piva

Location
Matera, Italy

Area
5,000 m²

Photography
Andrea Martiradonna

La Suite is a five-star hotel designed by Studio Marco Piva, located in a strategic area in the historic centre of Matera, with two impressive views: the city's most important street, the famous Via Lucana, and a courtyard space for collective activities for city residents and visitors.

A Traditionally Modern Complex

The uniqueness of this five-star structure lies in the synaesthesia of aspects that pertain, on the one hand, to the social and urban fabric of the context, and on the other hand, to the analysis of contemporary stylistic trends, giving rise to a traditionally modern complex.

Pure and elegant in form, with its essential fluid spaces and expression of functional architecture, La Suite Hotel presents itself as a triumphant building, whose design is intuitively inspired by the twentieth-century current of Italian rationalism, characterised by a lack of decorations to promote an authenticity that concretely integrates into the historical city.

Winter Garden Filter the Outside and Inside

The Hotel is designed to offer an exclusive stay thanks to its formal fineness, the use of local materials and the renovation of an imposing arched portal of the 17th century, which characterises the entrance to the building with its strong presence. The symbolism of the arch, an archetypal element that reminds of the Tuff caves of the Civita, is just one of the many iconic elements that characterize this structure and create a line of continuity with the past.

The charming Winter Garden, a real seamless extension, acts as a filter between the outside and the inside and that can be enjoyed every time of the year. The architectural study of the facade is undoubtedly original, marked by the juxtaposition of vertically arranged, chromatically calm lighting elements, which define a new, visibly homogeneous space with warm colours, in contrast to the intense light the city reflects naturally.

An overall view of the fragmented facade is also offered by the rhythmic position of the Mazzaro slabs which is a very resistant and performing type of Tuff, and is also used as a traditional local covering material.

Elegant Details Bring Timeless Style

La Suite consists of 40 generously sized rooms of different surface areas, equipped with flexible spaces, customised furniture, including lamps at bed heads, and bathrooms, characterised by a homogeneous chromaticism that reminds of domesticity. The building comprises a basement and six floors above ground; on the ground floor there are the hall, the coffee bar and the breakfast room, which can be converted into an informal meeting space. In the basement, there is a meeting room, a spa comprising a wellness centre and a fitness room, and finally a wine cellar for tasting fine wines.

There is also the large lounge and the panoramic terraces that open onto the city, creating a versatile place, a new point of urban sociality and expression of modern human needs, marked by the desire to know the urban fabric in which they are found.

The wide spaces are characterized by plays of perspective, iconic elements and by a scenic use of light. Geometries, volumes and materials, from the most technical ones in flooring, to structural laminates, to traditional stones, are expressed through fine workmanship and elegant details, creating a timeless style.

The atmosphere is made welcoming in all areas of the hotel, including common areas and rooms; it has been thought to provide visual relaxation for human eyes, used to the cold and artificial lights of the city.

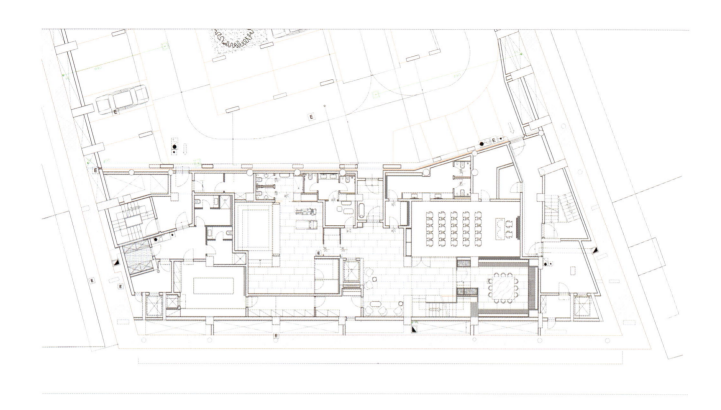

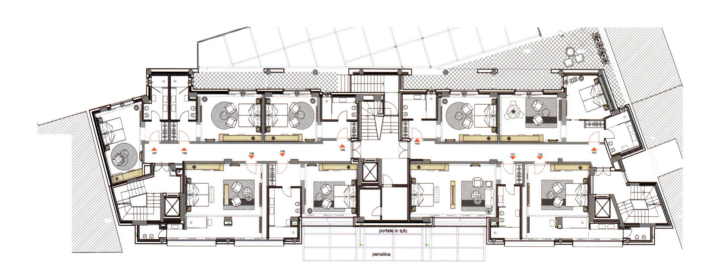

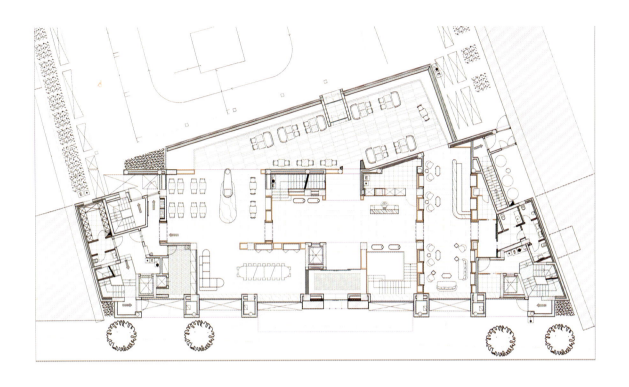

083

Hotel Space

Hotel Ease

Design Agency
ARTTA Concept Studio

Location
Hong Kong, China

Photography
Peter Cheung

Hotel Ease, initially a commercial building now transformed into a Teahouse-like hotel, now is located in Kwai Chung. The design concept of Hotel Ease is inspired by the 1920's of New York City — the commercial heart of America, with the growing of businessmen, traders and planters. The city has impressed people with profession so large that the amount of quality lodging establishments began to emerge. This inspiration is to create a unique and relaxing experience for the customers that stay in Hong Kong.

Go Back the Past New York with Art Deco Style

Art Deco has a distinguished style of simple and clean lines with bold geometric forms. This can be seen on the lobby flooring; using black patterned marble arranged in handcrafted planks to create a dynamic look. In addition, paintings, bicycles, vintage suitcases and cameras have been arranged to give it an authentic look and to make guests feel as if they have stepped back in time to New York City.

In addition to bringing New York City inside Hotel Ease, the project also gave support to local art development. To achieve this aim, the corridors on each floor have been turned into an art gallery, featuring works by local artists.

An example of abstract in this interior can be seen behind the reception. The square frame decor is made of brass stainless steel — slim, straight and tough. A combination of delicacy and harshness emphasize the professions of New York. The unique silver-grey timber veneer is the main wall-finishing that surrounds the interior, as it is visually shinny and carries the raw texture of wood grain, transforming the place into a high-end hotel.

Bring in Nature

This hotel has a nature theme and to capture this essence, the designers used planter boxes around the hotel to bring nature inside from the outside and create a warm and cosy atmosphere.

Designers also bring in different elements such as concrete, wood and matte with less reflection so that the rooms would have a balanced and comfortable atmosphere. They have used wooden colours combined with shades of grey and white for a neutral atmosphere. With a mixture of materials such as carpet and concrete juxtaposed with unique patterns around the decor enhances a modern and stylish hotel.

The rooms are furnished with a combination of black, white and navy blue. A formal colour palette that can be associated with professionals is to create a classic and elegant ambiance. The room numbers are designed in a unique font for a touch of Deco. Furthermore, the sink basin has been placed outside the bathroom and within the bedroom so that it is convenient for the guests.

1ST FLOOR

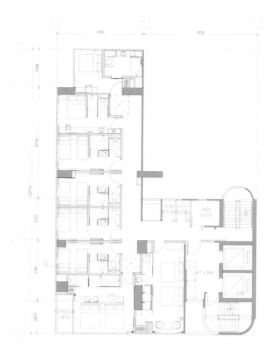

3RD FLOOR

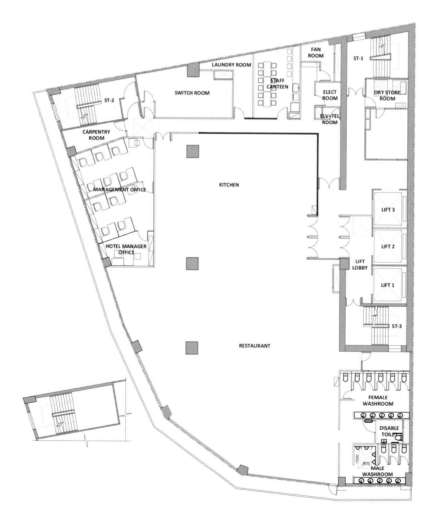

MP LEVEL 1 MASTER LAYOUT PLAN
1:200

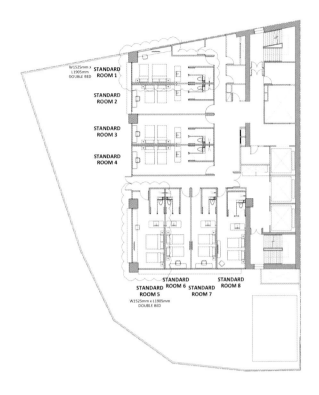

MP LEVEL 3 MASTER LAYOUT PLAN
1:200

MP UG MASTER LAYOUT PLAN
1:200

Hotel Space

Can Bordoy Grand House & Garden

Design Agency:
OHLAB / Paloma Hernaiz, Jaime Oliver

Location:
Palma de Mallorca, Spain

Photography:
José Hevia

Can Bordoy Grand House & Garden, located in the heart of the historic centre of Palma de Mallorca, is a small hotel with 24 rooms, a magnificent garden, swimming pool, spa and panoramic terrace. Can Bordoy is a house that has suffered many renovations throughout its more than 500 years of history. It is not a noble building that has faithfully followed the historical traditions of its time but quite the opposite. This is a house that has passed through many hands, and has had many interventions, sometimes aggressive and often breaking the cultural and historical conventions of its time in an (arguably) fortunate way.

Respect the Patina of the Passage of Time

The project designed and carried out by OHLAB and developed by Mikael Hall and his family, is a respectful intervention with that architectural crossbreeding, maintaining the traces of the past and avoiding a false recovery of a glorious past that the house has never had.

The architects are inspired by the principles of the traditional Japanese technique of Kintsugi — the art of repairing broken antique porcelain with a precious material, such as gold dust, and thus obtaining a repaired piece that does not hide the fracture, but shows it and celebrates it and whose result is a piece that may have even more value than the ceramic before breaking. OHLAB does not pretend to hide the heterodox eclecticism of the existing building, but instead conciliates and celebrates the different layers of history and clearly highlights the new interventions that have been necessary to give the house its new use.

The first step was to analyse the different construction phases of the building, to select and protect the most distinct elements for their protection. The next stage was to restore, replace and complete the missing parts from original pieces of the different eras. A simple palette of materials that respect the existing architecture was used, such as lime mortar, traditional stucco plaster and noble stone. Where possible, old elements have also been salvaged to integrate the installations and structures in a subtle way.

Evoke the Experience of Visiting a House

Rather than being at a hotel reception, the clients meet at the entrance hall of the house. At the entrance, a thin mirror, deformed into an ellipse by the structure of a staircase impossible to reproduce today, reinforces the structure of the stair and frames the reflection of the visitor entering the building as the new ephemeral protagonist of the house.

In the entrance hall, a mirror ceiling hides the new installations and doubles the height of the bar and the velvet curtain that surrounds it. In the main staircase, the skylight is flooded with water becoming a small pool with a transparent bottom that creates a play of light through the water, flooding the staircase with caustic reflections. The new section of stairs that is needed to connect the last floor has been designed with a modern steel structure covered in mirror finished steel cladding making its exterior disappear but also duplicating the caustic reflections through the stairwell while the interior of the staircase is finished with a warm and robust walnut. On the floor of the staircase, a circular glass embedded in the slab connects with the spa located in the basement and allows the spa user in the basement to see the sky through the water plane on the roof.

Outstanding Bespoke Furniture Reflects the Eclecticism of the Architecture

The furniture is from very different eras and origins. You can find old pieces that OHLAB together with the owner Mikael Hall have been compiling for this project during more than two years. European antiques from Paris, Copenhagen, Stockholm, Istanbul, are combined with pieces from different antique shops in Mallorca, handcrafted pieces of the island such as the Gordiola lamps, elements found in the existing house, as well as some pieces of the new owner's private collection. These antiques coexist with contemporary furniture from the likes of GTV Thonet, Baxter, Moroso, Artemide, Norr, Santa & Cole, and Flos, carefully selected.

The bed, with its bedside tables and headboards finished in walnut and velvet and equipped with bespoke aged brass lamps and brass pushbuttons, form a delicate and intimate space that contrasts with the rough and unfinished texture of the existing walls and ceilings. A different model of bar in all rooms is another sophisticated comfort element with an integrated mini bar, fridge, snack pantry, extendable table, lighting and built-in Audio Pro sound system, as well as a very easy to use custom-made old-fashioned brass button table.

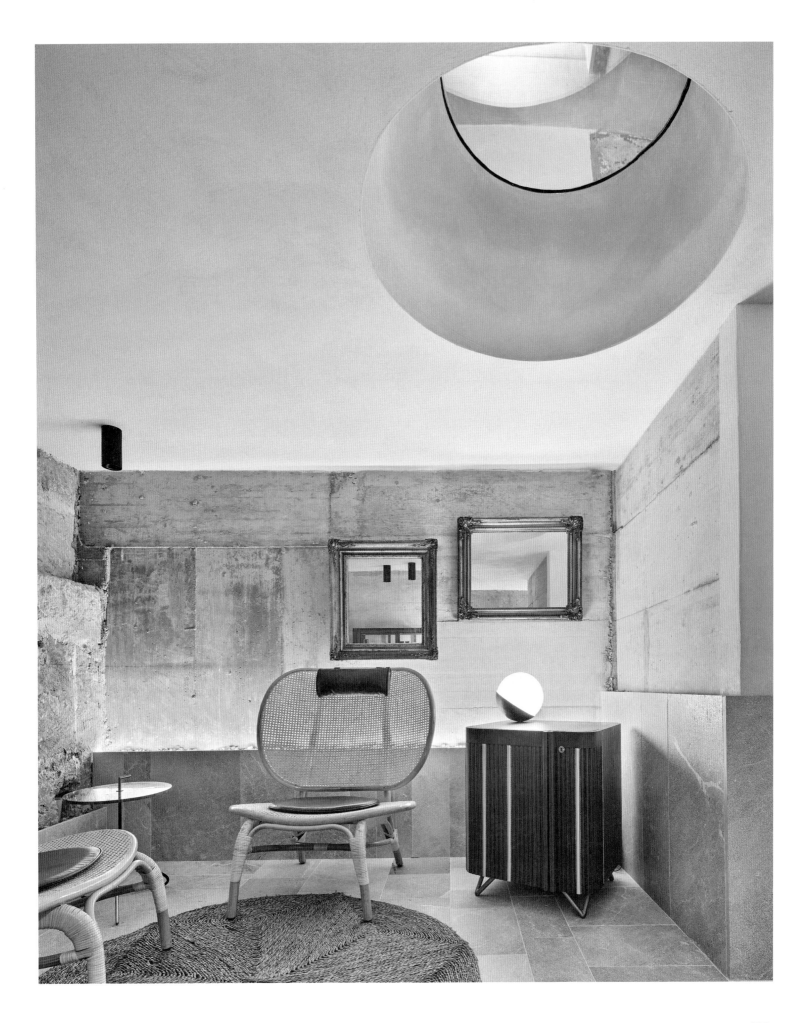

Hotel Space

Cretan Malia Park

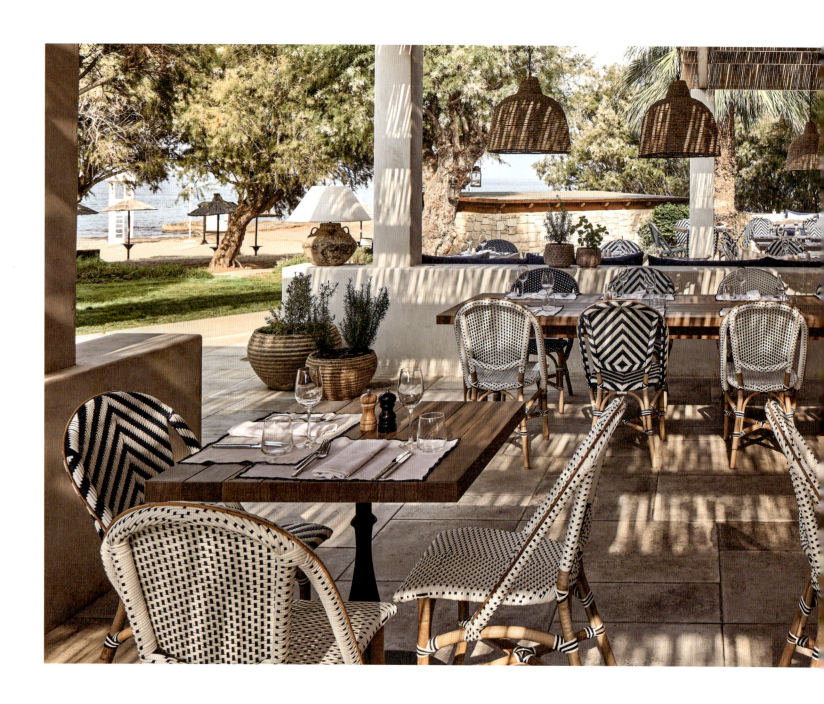

Design Agency:
Vana Pernari Architecture Studio

Location:
Crete, Greece

Client:
Phaea Resorts

Photography:
Claus Brechenmacher & Reiner Baumann

Cretan Malia Park is a flora-filled retreat that augments classic Aegean hospitality with a focus on refined luxury and slow-paced living on Crete's Malia coastline. Owned by the Sbokos family since it opened in the 1980s, the 204-room hotel has undergone an extensive renovation program led by Greek architect Vana Pernari, that was inspired by the colours and textures of the island and the Mediterranean Sea.

The Mediterranean Colour Palette

The architect aimed to incorporate the Mediterranean colour palette as described in Van Gogh's quote — "The Mediterranean has the colour of mackerel, changeable I mean. You don't always know if it is green or violet, you can't even say it's blue, because the next moment the changing reflection has taken on a tint of rose or grey." — as found in the murals of the ancient Minoan cities in Crete as well as in the local folk art.

The hotel's exteriors have been stripped back to reveal an exquisitely simple canvas that both references the island's architectural heritage and allows for the resort's verdant gardens to take centre stage. Tonal, rough-hewn walls are framed by local swaying palms, banana trees, and Indian figs and oversized windows further delineate indoor and outdoor areas.

The intrinsic relationship with the surroundings extends to the resort's interiors, which are defined by the use of natural materials such as walnut, chestnut, and bamboo. The ever-changing colours of the Mediterranean landscape are reflected in the use of rattan, stone, brass and ceramics, which combine to impart a warm, relaxed mood in the light-filled public spaces and guestrooms.

A Mixture of Exotic and Local Design

From a sculptural, monolithic reception desk to an American Indian inspired artwork made of tiles on the wall behind it, from mid-century modern furniture to macramé pendant lamps and other boho elements, from brutalist coffee tables to luxe British textiles and Provence handwoven wicker floor lamps.

The stylistic legacy of Crete, both past and present, is explored through a blend of modern art, family heirlooms, and custom pieces crafted by local artisans; flora-inspired artworks, thoughtful details such as the hand-made herringbone cement tiles and the locally sourced ceramic pots. Beyond the contemporary Cretan design concept, the hotel plays host to a roll call of high-end design names — including GUBI, House of Hackney, Børge Mogensen, 101 Copenhagen and LRNCE— to form a range of looks from mid-century modern to laidback boho.

For example, the hotel's rooms and suites are defined by their own set of decorative markers. Double guestrooms are characterized by herringbone flooring and geometrically styled jade-hued wall tiles, while the light and airy bungalows are punctuated with shots of blue or terracotta, applied by way of graphic wall tiling and textiles. In the suites, bespoke sideboards, wardrobes and folding doors accented with rattan screens introduce a rustic fringe to otherwise contemporary spaces.

This hotel has three places to enjoy food. The first one is Mouries, which is a large patio for traditional Cretan cuisine. A display of tomato preserves, a small herbs garden, large Cretan baskets, and a functional firewood oven create a feeling of a homey Cretan courtyard. The second is Almyra for Italian cuisine which sits by the blue waters of the Mediterranean Sea and under a large pitched wooden pergola, with white-washed walls on a terracotta floor and concrete sofas in blue and white hues evoke the feeling of an authentic Italian seafront setting. The third one is a relaxed beach shack bar which sits right by the beach. Under large rattan umbrellas as well as comfy daybeds, guests can lay back and enjoy the sunset.

An Extension of a Traditional Cretan Yard

In the lobby, the sculptural reception desk features a solid pleated top made of red marble and a brass monolithic leg. Next to the reception stands a sculptural desk for the guest relation manager, custom made of smoked oak and brass details and a large artwork by Philippos Theodoridis on the brushed concrete column behind it.

The lobby bar in the centre adds colour to the space with a combination of turquoise Gio-Ponti inspired tiles along with rust-red handmade Moroccan concrete tiles — a tribute to the rich ceramic tradition around the Mediterranean Sea. The space is filled with green, both in large planters in several pots and on the walls, where sustainably-preserved plants are placed, and creating vertical garden-like installations.

A large walnut wood bookcase frames two windows creating a small reading area right in front of them, while a large walnut table and two cosy areas around it invite the guests to explore the hotel's library, read, interact or even work. At seating, many different textiles are combined, from white and floral linens to rust red and mustard yellow velvets to natural leathers.

Diversified Entertainment Space

A small gym and spa were converted from a small pitched-roof bungalow sheltered amongst the famed local banana trees in the resort's yard. The architect have also redesigned Kids' Club which is nestled in a bungalow in the resort's lush gardens, the light-filled interior includes a kitchen with a large island for cooking & baking activities and a large playing area with a large display that can be adapted to many different kids' activities, such as painting and crafts as well as dancing and theatre lessons. A separate youth club, exclusively designed for teenagers, features a large water tub and tall trees with hammocks; an exclusive bar and a cinema screen; while table tennis, billiards, darts and other activities keep teens busy by the day. The place transforms itself to an atmospheric ambiance with hanging moon lights, poufs and cinema screenings by night.

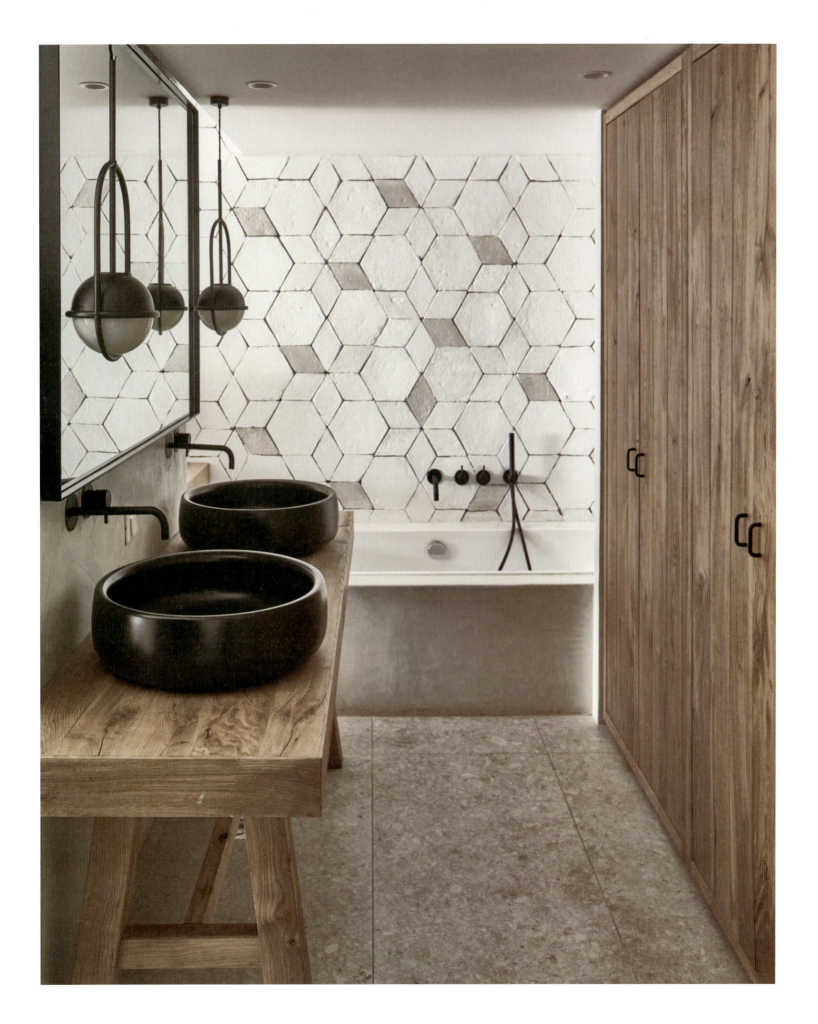

3

RESIDENTIAL SPACE

Residential Space

Albert Court Apartment

Design Agency
Teresa Sapey + Partners

Location
London, UK

Area
667 m²

Photography
Asier Rua

Located in a 19th century mansion in London, England, the ALBERT COURT apartment is a high-class residential project completed by Madrid-based design agency Teresa Sapey + Partners. The designers have combined two adjoining flats into a single residential space. The mere clash of lines and colours builds a bright and elegant space.

Spatial or Soul, at Least One is Flowing

To a certain extent, art is interlinked. The owner is a professional sculpture artist who has been developing in his field since he graduated from the collage. A space is just like the sculpture. An excellent sculpture lies in its soul, like Michelangelo's *David*, like Alessandro's *Milo's Venus*, like Auguste Rodin's *Thinker*, etc. These are all works of art devoted to the author's efforts. They are all works of art with their soul, which have remained unchanged for thousands of years.

He is an artist with deep thought. The villa owners don't plan to live for a long time, it is like a club, a relaxing place or a place to create inspiration. Through space planning, material control and colour matching, they can build a space that can communicate with nature and integrate into the environment.

In terms of the function of the interior space, the designer did not think the need to fill all the space, he wanted this to be a living room, a spiritual space, a living space, therefore, in the dimensional layout, the designer used a lot of white, intentionally allowing the tones of the outside environment to fill in the gaps and bring the whole space to life.

Quiet Oriented Colour Schemes

On the material, considering the owner not live for a long time, to keep the indoor material not affected by the temperature of the surrounding environment and humidity, the designers have done a lot of investigation to understand the relationship between materials and the environment, to solve the important influencing factors to the space. The designer takes advantage of scenes to extent the "liquidity" and "extensity" of each living space, in order to create different visual effects in different season and time. Designers fluently used the abstract design such as "deconstruction", "fragmentation" and "rhythm", to break the solidification synaesthesia of household space. The designer wants to express that the sense of "unknown" of life is full of possibilities and release the daily household functions required.

In terms of colour, the concept adopted by the designer is environment oriented and quite oriented. There is only one protagonist here, that is, the rare primitive natural environment in the noisy city. We need to weaken the boundary between the architectural space and the environment, so that we can be more integrated into the natural environment, feel more peace in our hearts, and achieve the ultimate goal of this design. It is the source of creative inspiration to focus on rest. Therefore, in terms of colour, the designer mainly uses black and white grey to express, with a small amount of green plants and red books to embellish, so that the whole space will not appear rigid.

Residential Space

Kennedy Residence

Design Agency

Guillaume Alan

Location

Paris, France

Photography

Matthew Donaldson

The apartment is in a magnificent early 19th century haussmannian edifice, with views on the Seine and the Eiffel Tower. The couple worked and traveled a lot, always spending time in very nice places all around the world. They have the following four requirements for the project: firstly, the project had to be amazing, in surprising them but also in achieving serene and calm atmosphere, accordingly to their needs. Secondly, meeting the same high standard levels than hotels and villas where they visit. Thirdly, to make a place of livability and fun. Finally, it's a place where the homeowners, who have a passion for wine, organize cocktails and parties, a festive place. As the designer said, "it's all about restrain in architecture and elements but opulent in spirit".

Minimalist and Clean

Inspired by history, the designer's core concept is minimalism, a complete reorganization of the space has been made. Light has been extremely important in terms of architecture: it's an element they've tried to understand at the very first steps of the project. Light makes architecture, it's thanks to the light that walls, space, shadows can exist. The entrance hall — inspired by the Orangery in Versailles — designer created a series of high ceiling stone arches with recessed mirrors. The old mosaic floor has been kept with its beautiful, degraded tones of greys, bronze and old gold.

The living room is a brilliant example of Guillaume Alan signature: the way how he treats and defines space is very clean. Vaults have been drawn to create a magnificent and unusual height ceiling, the large window has been drawn, inspired by an old door in Oxford in England. The fireplace with its 3 m length has been carved inside a huge piece of natural Carrare marble and gives the feeling of floating in the air, in weightlessness and gives the impression to be liquid and as if it has flowed down on the floor, creating lines crossing each other's and as if it had spread through all the apartments. As for the dining room, the style is instantly recognizable: strong lines, impeccable proportions balanced with douceur brought by curved lines of the furniture and soft textures and palette.

Palette and Textures

The palette here is monochrome, all about degraded shades, in a very light grey palette. We created it and we call it "craie" (chalk) colour. All the rooms in the apartment are linked with same materials and palette. The palette weaves through different supports: walls (bespoke painting), floor (light grey brushed oak and natural marble lines), brushed ash wood, rug in natural linen, leather, silk, wool...

The same natural Carrare marble is used through all the architecture in the apartment (lines in the floor, fireplace, mid- height walls, bathroom...). Also, example of how furniture pieces arose from projects and how they are totally connected with architecture: the legs of the table kitchen are in same brushed ash wood used through all the apartment and same marble for the tabletop. Very sensitive and poetic work on the space. It's all about luxury and radicality because no ornament or superfluous. But all is perfectly balanced with softness brought by the hand-crafted ash wood textured doors, soft paint, linen rug and heavy linen curtains.

Although this gorgeous apartment isn't shy of space, by using the same tone across the apartment not only creates the illusion of more space but it also allows for more depth, texture and warmth to be added to each room without needed to commit to a colour or unneeded feature.

French Furniture Pieces

All the furniture pieces have been thought, drawn by the same hand, designer is signing here the project in harmony with the finest tradition of French design and Décorateurs Ensembliers. Designer knows how to add subtlety and douceur by offering interiors and furniture pieces that are understated and based on luxury architecture and fabrication. For this home, these include a very meticulous selection of materials, a choice, made with passion of: marble with its delicate and poetic grain: every vein was chosen to be in the right pattern, woods and their grains, never identical, together with finishes on samples that are fine-tuned to perfection before being implemented in the finished object.

It's always a quest for perfection and excellence based on tradition and craftsmanship with creativity, sensitivity and poetry. Very proud of this project, it's flawless and harmonious, a very poetic project, without ostentation. Purity is a way of life.

Residential Space

Show Apartment "Shades Of Grey"

Design Agency
Ippolito Fleitz Group

Location
Shanghai, China

Client
CEG Schwarzwald

Photography
Sui Sicong

This project is a flat in the "Schwarzwald" building, developed by the Chinese Eagle Group (CEG) and designed by Ippolito Fleitz Group (IFG). Many metropolitans are longing for a place of tranquillity and relaxation where their families might adopt a healthy and sustainable lifestyle. Amidst a forest of 20,000 trees, the "Schwarzwald" apartment towers offer the unique synthesis of living a modern urban life in a quality environment.

As its name suggests, the central theme of the "Shades of Grey" show apartment focuses on a full range of grey nuances. With its elegant and meditative calm, the apartment would perfectly suit a globetrotter's desires after a long and tiring trip. Layers and interactions of premium materials, fascinating textures and high-contrast surfaces turn this 250 m^2 apartment into a metropolitan sanctuary with a breath-taking view of Shanghai's skyline.

A Space Rich in Subtle Grey Variations

Upon entering the apartment, a piece of art in green tones instantly attracts the visitor's attention. A spacious living-dining area with an integrated floor-to-ceiling kitchen extends across the entire apartment width. From the balcony on the north side, through the interior and all the way to the horizon on the opposing side, nothing in the apartment blocks the clear view. A painted aluminium slat ceiling both zones the living-dining area and creates a cosy atmosphere through indirect lighting. Filigree and nearly invisible, a glass shelve separates the dining table from a spacious couch arrangement and offers space for memories.

Herringbone-patterned parquet flooring in dark grey literally lays the foundation for the "Shades of Grey" theme, whereas contrasting hues of green and blue create highlights and support the apartment's modern, elegant and calm atmosphere. The contrasting, yet matching mix of materials creates an atmosphere of both calm intimacy and excitement in the living area. Here, layered carpets meet fabrics with exciting haptic features and smooth marble and mirror-glass surfaces, while earth and gold-toned accessories provide an extra touch of luxury. Merely separated from the living area by ceiling-high glass, there is a small, half-open workspace with a comfortable sofa corner.

Warm shades of grey, natural wooden surfaces, indirect lighting and luxuriant fabrics tastefully contrast with the bedrooms' smooth surfaces and create a relaxed ambience. Thanks to a sophisticated combination of vivid marble grains, unpretentious white sanitary items and accessories in black and gold, the bathrooms unfold in an aura of classic and timeless taste. With "Shades of Grey" this project invites you into the beautiful and diverse world of grey nuances.

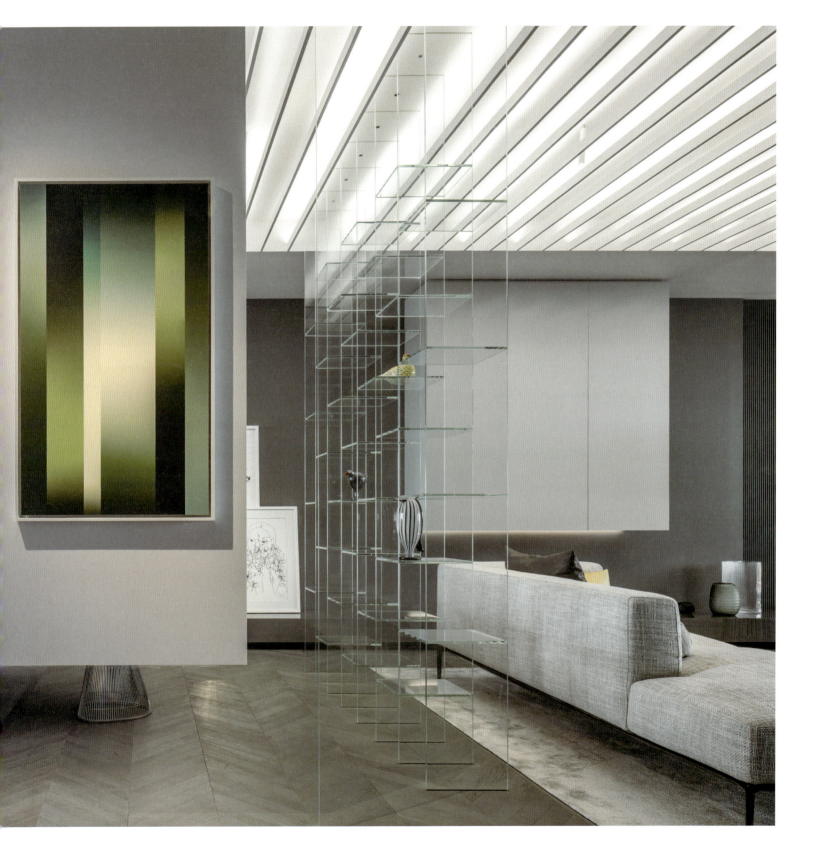

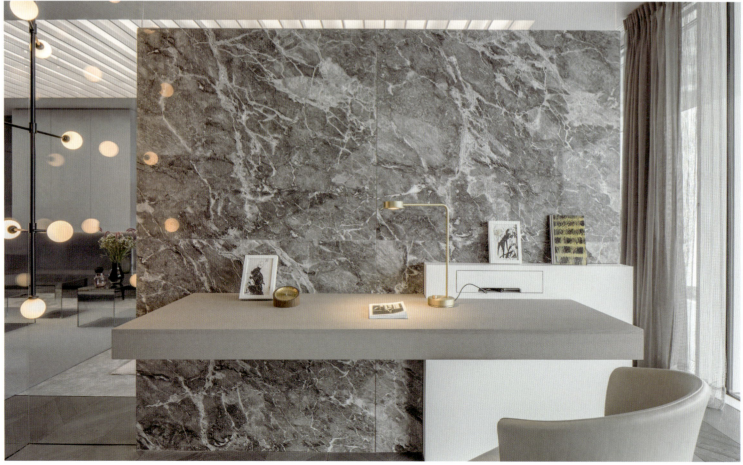

Residential Space

Serenity In The City

Design Agency
Peny Hsieh Interiors

Location
Taiwan, China

Area
310 m²

Photography
Hey!Cheese

A serene view from the top of the house strengthens the busyness of the city. All come into view. A great contrast and comparison are formed between the busyness of city and serenity of the room; they are conflicted yet connected at the same time. It's a lifestyle, a beautiful balance between fast and slow, move and still, busy and leisure in our life. It's an attitude for our life, and a beginning of design: an inspiration from the outdoor and the primal nature emphasize the slow lifestyle.

Serene Stones and Leisure in the City

From the entryway, the facade and ceiling extend the three-dimensional lines, and the subtly embedded light source stretch out like streams flowing out of seams. Turning around, we could see a paradise before us: the wide living room takes grey as the basic hue, revealing the truth of life by the primal texture; wavy arches ripple on the ceiling; an impressive screen wall depicts a levelled vision of landscape; black window frames and walls create scenery where conversation between the inside and the outside is formed.

The greenery of the garden in the air is an energy that smoothes our life, bringing leisure and rumination to this project. The aisle adapts the image of outdoor brick walls, connected to the main bedroom space on the other end. It's also a harmonious interlude between public area and private serenity. The main bedroom is covered by two grey wooden cases, which form a warm hole along with the arch falling down from the top. The light slowly infiltrates through the window and the walls, speaking of an eternity. In the membrane of the inside and the outside, the busyness of city is simply a sigh beneath our feet, and the nature is only a step from us. A breeze blows from the landscape. Relieving our heart, a deep but calm force brings the din away.

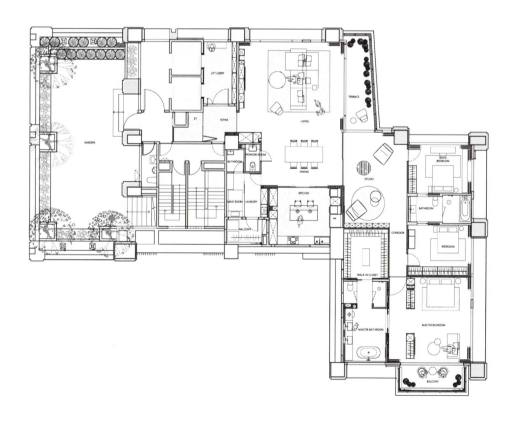

Residential Space

Modern Zen

Design Agency
ZRIVERSTUDIO

Location
New York, USA

Area
120 m²

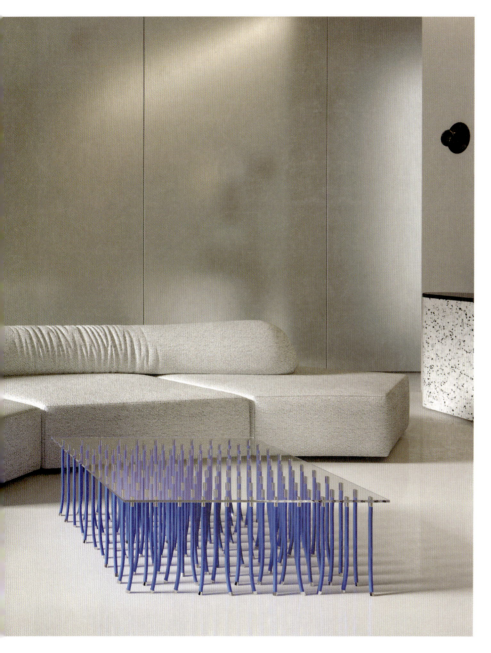

In a noisy, densely overpopulated modern world full of visual advertisements, non-recyclable materials, and excess of different objects people need to find own Modern Zen. This project is about introversion, digital detox, reflections on purity, mindfulness of choice. It makes us think about what surrounds us and who we are. Confronting the informational squall, we want to have a visually clean interior. We feel the desire to find calm and peace in the midst of noise.

Modern Zen is an apartment with spectacular views over the ultra-modern metropolis — New York. The possession of more and more material things is no longer perceived as a guarantee of happiness. Seeking a shelter does not mean a categorical rejection of objects. It is a matter of clearly formulated appreciation, functional design objects and only high-quality concepts. Limiting the speed of our lives implies a desire to find a "shelter" in the house and digital detox.

Splendid Selection of Furniture

In a minimalist space, the furniture fittings become the focal point of the whole project. The central element of the living room is biomorphic and monolithic sofa "On the Rocks" by Edra in white wool. In front of the sofa is Org table in electric blue by Cappellin, a famous Italian furniture brand, and behind the sofa is a cactus decor sculpted from stone. The general space of the apartment is formed on one side by metal wall panels which denote technogenicity and a futuristic direction. The surrounding space is obscured, revealing another dimension of the interior to the observer.

The chair near the window side is Roly-Poly Chair designed by Faye Too Good, smooth and rounded with a maternal glow and can be customised in original, charcoal and cream colours. The Roly-Poly chair is now in the permanent collections of museums around the world, such as the Philadelphia Museum of Art, the Denver Art Museum and the National Gallery of Victoria, for its unique design concept.

At the centre of the kitchen is a large dining table from the famous Italian furniture brand Cassina, surrounded by three Swan Chairs by Rick Owens. Hanging from the top are W151 Extra Large pendant from Swedish lighting brand Wästberg, whose products take on the simplest of lines and design concepts, rough but endearing and full of industrial aesthetic appeal.

In the bedroom, one is instantly drawn to "Ekstrem" Lounge Chair by Terje Ekström, which represents Norwegian post-modern design. The individual design breaks out of the traditional furniture box and combines aesthetics and ergonomics without compromising on comfort. In the white space, Bold side table by Destroyers and the Angel Wing floor lamp look less conspicuous. A simple floor lamp is designed by Alvar Aalto, one of the founding fathers of Scandinavian style, for Artek in 1954.

A painting by Lucio Fontana hangs on the wall, which pokes holes in the canvas, breaking the two-dimensional knot and creating another dimension.

Decorated with Paintings Full of Stories

In addition to the furniture, the paintings create the atmosphere for meditation and thinking, for example, the photographs of Dutch photographer Hendrik Kerstens. Hendrik is best known for his photographs of his daughter Paula, whose composition and colour textures are reminiscent of 17th century Dutch portraiture. Combining elements of the past and present, this whimsical design gives the character to the interior, makes it futuristic and mysterious.

In the bathroom, hangs painting "Bag" by Hendrik Kerstens (2007) on the wall. This portrait of his daughter Paula was made as an ecological comment on the number of plastic bags given away by shops, which has become the source of many fashion designers' lids.

The Kangaroo Chair designed by Pierre Jeanneret is placed casually and the North floor lamp next to the bath is from the Spanish lighting brand Vibia, one of the best local brands with recognisable lamps designed to fit a variety of spaces.

4

OFFICE SPACE

Office Space

Artek Headquarter Helsinki

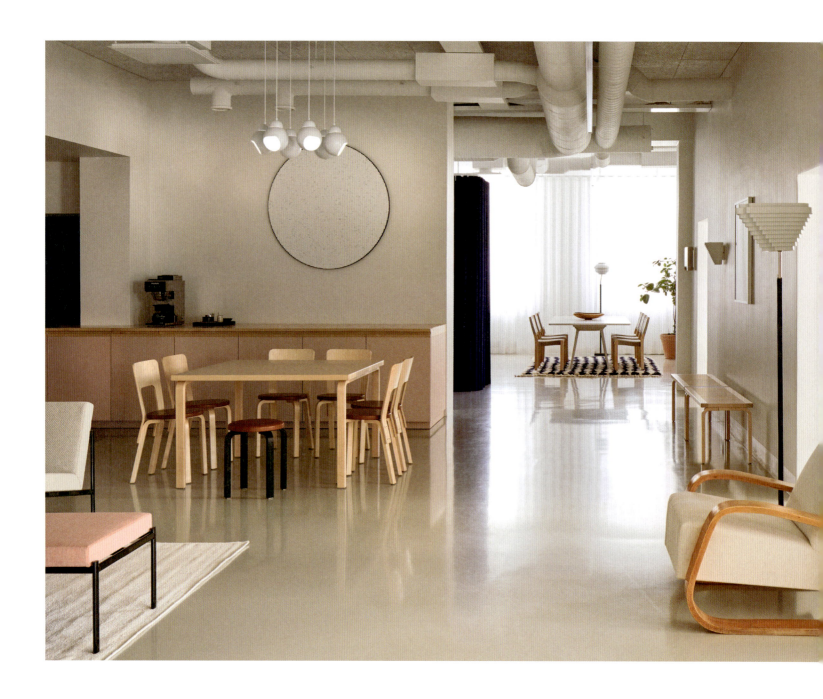

Design Agency
Sevil Peach

Location
Helsinki

Area
470 m²

Photography
Tuomas Uusheimo

Artek's new premises are situated on the 4th floor of a converted elegant 19th century apartment building, located in the city centre and opposite the iconic Stockmann department store. Whilst serving as Artek's headquarter, the new office should also act as a "working showroom" for architects and dealers. The new environment therefore has to achieve multiple goals: to convey the "Artek Spirit" through the planning and use of materials, to create a democratic environment with maximum daylight, and to demonstrate the right balance between Artek and Vitra products.

Designed to allow the users to work in a varied way, the workplace flexibly suits their task in hand and their mood. Whilst they are provided with dedicated desks, users are encouraged to use the entire environment: to work comfortably on the sofa; to sit at the informal meeting table; to sit or stand. At the centre of the office, the spacious social hub fosters communication and impromptu meetings, invites for touchdown work and is flexibly furnished to allow for events to be hosted.

The "Blank" Space

With a fast-track programme of seven months from start to completion, the design process had to be highly efficient. The challenging schedule affected the choice of materials used. Although some finishes appear raw and "as found". A seamless industrial poured floor finish is introduced to all areas. Its neutral grey tone blends in with the roughly textured acoustic strand boards used underneath the structural soffit.

The primary goal was to strip the space back to its bare structure with the space being stripped back to its structural shell — a blank canvas which acts as a clean backdrop for the products and the activities. All the individual zones have become interconnected with beautiful vistas, including views to the outside. The designer striped the space. The 470 m² space is divided into a series of small rooms. All doors are omitted with the exception of meeting rooms and bathrooms. The sense of corridor is dissolved through a series of large and small openings. The enfilade creates a continuous perception of space and allows for easy and immediate communication between the various team spaces.

Five intimate human-scale work zones are supported by two meeting rooms. The central lounge area has an open kitchen with a library containing soft seating and a flexible layout dining table. In addition, facilities such as a sample library, chair rack, cloakroom, lockers, bathrooms and a copy print area complete the diverse office environment. Through the introduction of a seating bench, the rear corridor becomes a habitable place.

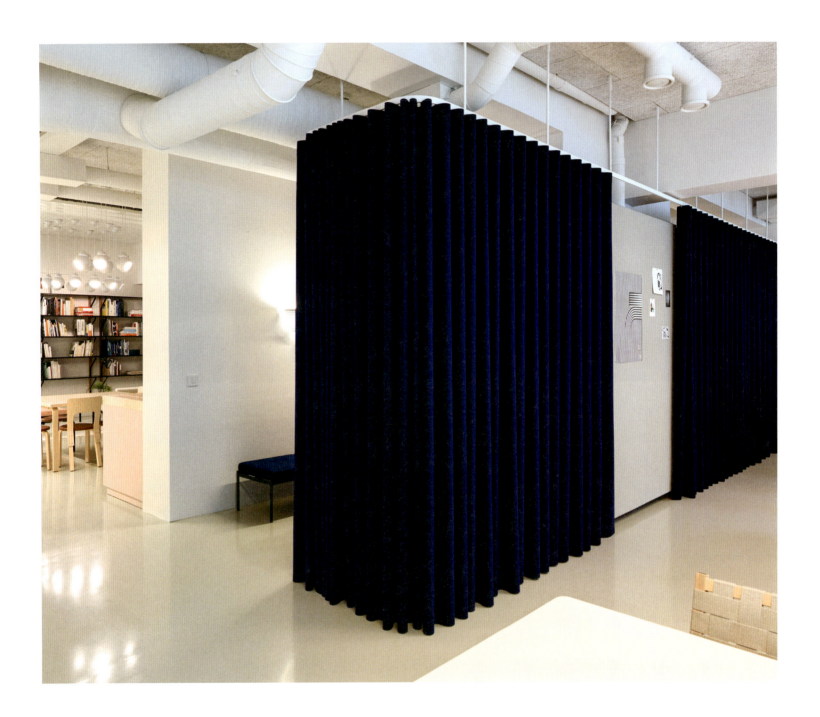

Variety of Colours

The white background of this case makes it easy for the designer to add various colours to the interior. Furthermore, the curtain colours provide an intuitive orientation throughout the space, as each zone has a different tone. The formal meeting room is wrapped with curtains that create a soft, embracing atmosphere whilst concealing presentation walls and providing good acoustics. Depending on whether the curtains are open or closed, the perception of the space can switch between that of a vivid workshop or a serene workplace. The "raw" atmosphere is enriched by the introduction of bold coloured curtains. These conceal and frame the sample library, chair display, storage, archive, lockers, write-on and pin-up boards. Improving the office acoustics through their softness, the curtains equally form a theatric setting to the functional galvanized steel shelving units behind. In order to maximise the ceiling height, all HVAC installations are exposed and painted white. The additional ceiling height and colour are used to create an open, light and airy environment.

The concept for the work environment is welcoming and friendly with a collage of furniture from Artek and Vitra. Whilst both companies have a strong DNA, their products effortlessly merge to create a harmonious contemporary interior. Linear Belux lights that are suspended slightly below the exposed HVAC installations create a bright yet restrained illumination. They are accompanied by a second light layer of decorative Artek light fittings which add a soft and homely ambiance to specific areas. Materials and details used for the purpose-made kitchen counter — lino fronts, birch handles and a tiled counter top — are a subtle homage to Artek's heritage and craftsmanship. Pieces from Artek's art collection are displayed throughout the space. The extensive book collection is housed in the central library, allowing employees as well as visitors to browse through decades of architecture, design and art.

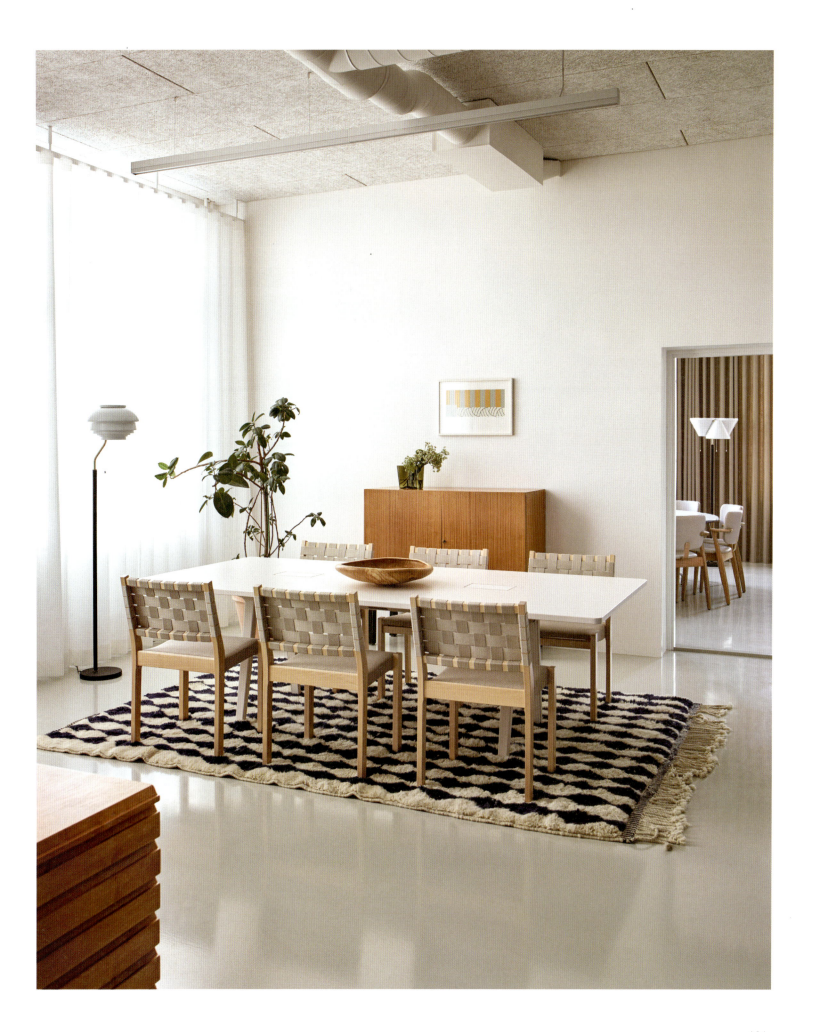

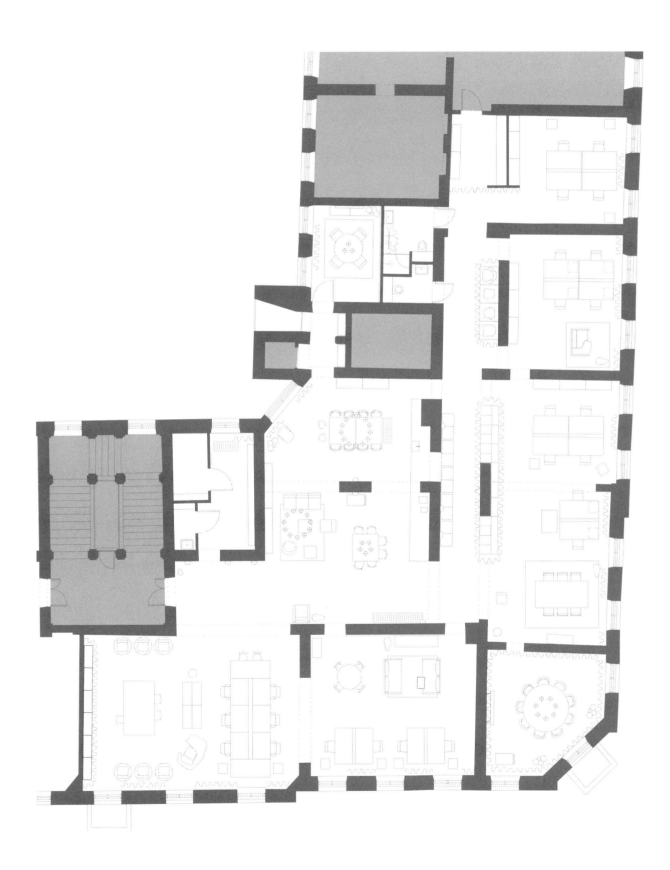

Office Space

Underwater Office

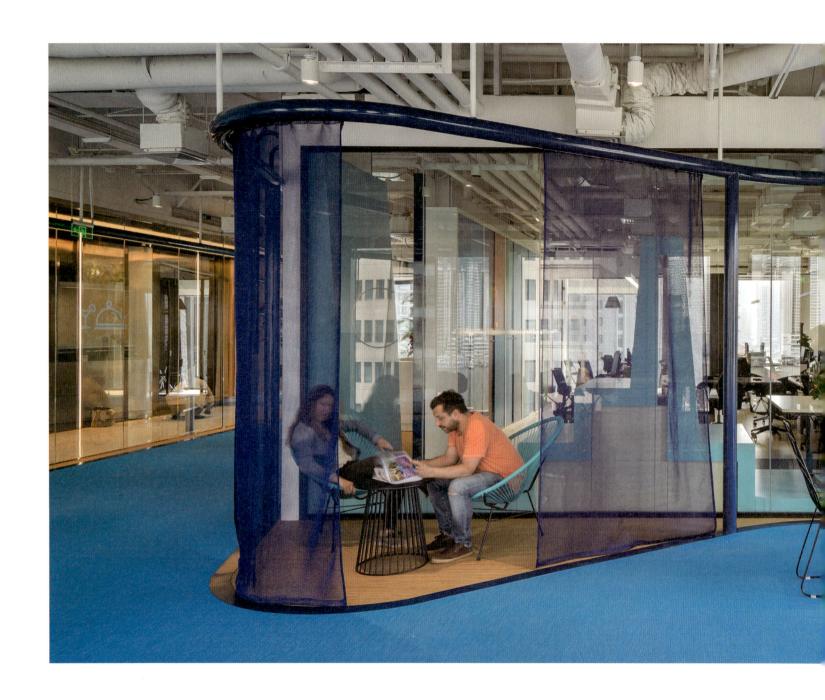

Design Agency
100architects

Location
Shanghai, China

Area
1,450 m²

Photography
Amey Kandalgaonkar

The "Underwater Office" is the new office of Club Med in Shanghai, a French prestige resort brand. Club Med is specialized in the market of all-inclusive holidays, with many vacation villages and resorts in the most exotic and breath-taking destinations around the World. From the very first meetings with them, they state very clearly that Club Med is an unconventional company, and their new office should reflect extravagancy, presenting themselves as a young & fresh company. Therefore, when brainstorming about the concept idea, the first thought in which the designers all agreed was to design an office that inspires vacations, holidays, and reflects the happiness that one feels when arriving to a new sunny destination at the sea.

Although the scope of work included the design of the entire office, Club Med specifically requested to have special accent in two main areas: the signature Lobby, which would be the space in charge of offering a very good first impression to clients and visitors alike; and the Pantry, which should be understood as a social space for employees, rather than just a pantry to have coffee or breakfast. Informal gatherings and team building activities were intended to take place in the social Pantry.

Greeting Customers at the Bottom of the Sea

Based on a Mediterranean feeling of holidays, which is swimming, the Lobby was conceptualized to mimic a swimming pool, in which visitors would be submerged under water. To create this illusion, a deep blue elevated pipe was designed to be hanging overheads, looping around the lobby defining different mini-areas within the lobby area. The shape of the pipe is at the same time projected onto the floor, in order to enhance the virtual subdivision of the space. The result is a multifunctional (but virtually subdivided) space in which each loop offers a mini-function, such as a reception desk, meeting room, waiting area, informal meeting spaces, hanging phone booths, etc. Two different design materials are used on either side of the pipe: blue PVC carpet as the pool water, and PVC wood flooring as the deck around the pool.

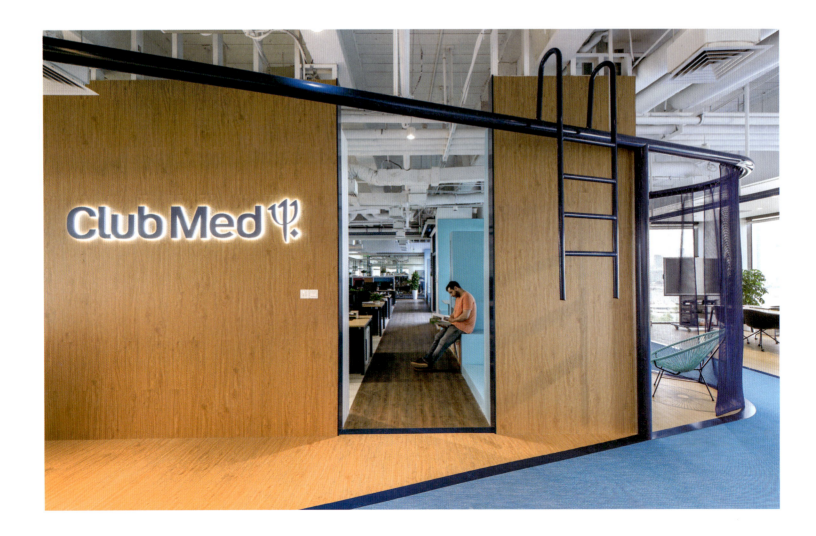

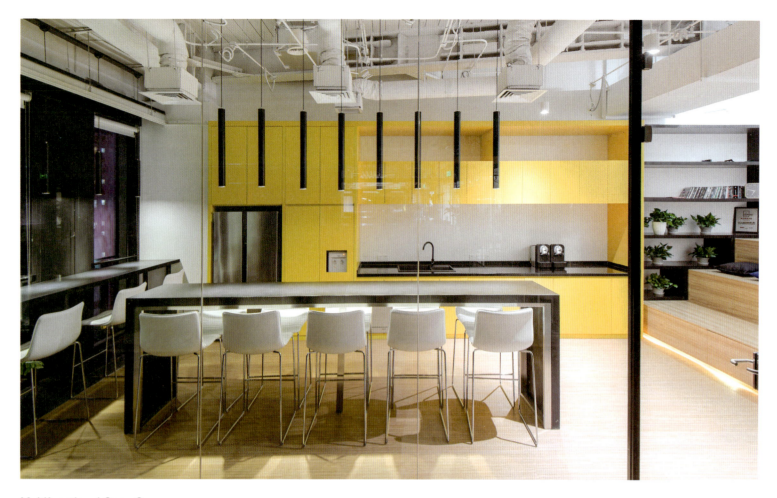

Multifunctional Open Space

The Pantry was designed to be as functional as possible having into account the diversity of activities that it would host. As main features, a long yellow kitchen was designed to solve all the practical needs of cooking, storing, coffee making, etc., in the same space, while a wooden mini-amphitheatre was located at the end of the space in order to provide enough seating areas for hosting communal activities or public speeches.

The working areas where solved with an open office typology, in order to foster relationships among employees and directors. Functionally, the workspaces feature not only long communal work desks, but also private offices with glass partitions that enhance transparency and bring natural light to all corners. Special mention for the two pieces of signature furniture designed for the open office in order to provide platforms for interactions among employees. Their morphology defines other mini-functions such as team briefings, small workshops, informal meetings, etc.

Office Space

Tencent Seafront Towers

Design Agency
B+H Architects

Location
Guangdong, China

Area
80,000 m²

Photography
Yijie Hu

Tencent's Seafront Towers is located in Shenzhen, Guangdong Province, and comprises a 248 m high south tower and a 194 m high north tower, known as the Twin Seafront Towers, which are the new city landmark of Shenzhen. B+H Architects adapts the concept of a vertical campus to offer amenities for work and play. The towers are connected by skybridges, where people moving between towers can interact and meet to create synergies and generate fresh ideas.

Creating a Vertical Community for Future Innovators

Tencent operates in a highly innovative industry where top talent is young, dynamic and smart. Client vision lies in promoting its global reach and creating a vibrant and collaborative work environment that fosters innovation, sparks creativity, and inspires staff.

Interiors are designed to harvest a close team culture in an unpretentious creative campus environment. The Tencent Academy is designed around a large daylight atrium. Designers applied indoor landscape at the base of the atrium, helping to filter air and to create an oasis for staff that spends most of their days at a computer or on their mobile phones. The knowledge link also houses training space, a dining hall, education centre, and meeting rooms. A wide range of settings for casual zones are provided. Flexible layouts with amenities that enable staff to easily reconfigure the space.

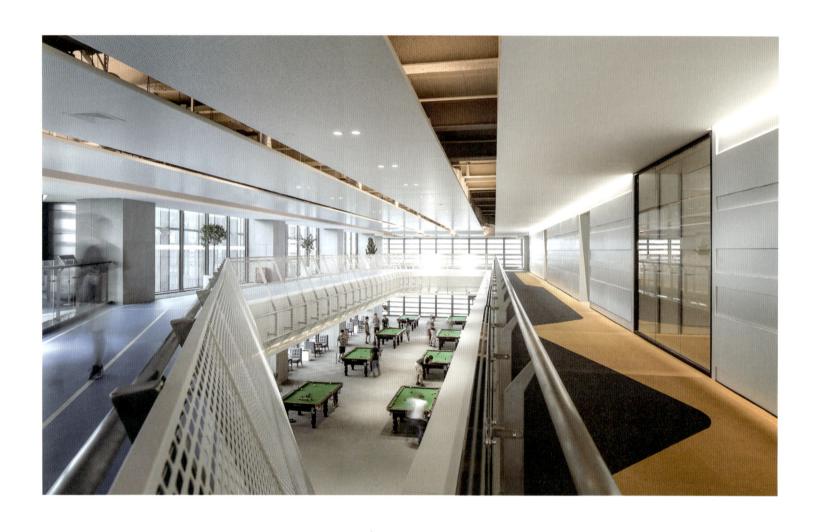

The atrium, designed as a vertical cliff, brings fresh air and daylight through a central skylight. The focal point is a vertical four-storey rock climbing wall. In the centre of the bridge lies a full basketball court, which can be turned into an event space for lectures, shows and concerts. Other features include a gym with panoramic views, ping pong tables, various play rooms, as well as a floor dedicated to meetings and conferences.

The design of swimming pool inspired by daybreak, the space is clad in a mosaic of tiles, forming an abstract image of clouds. A mirrored tensile fabric suspended from the ceiling reflects the water, pool and swimmers while helping to reflect natural light throughout the space.

Office Space

Sivantos Singapore

Design Agency
PLH Arkitekter A/S, Denmark

Location
Singapore

Photography
Owen Raggett

Sivantos headquarters in Singapore is a collaboration between Danish architecture practice PLH Arkitekter as the concept designer and workplace strategist, and local interior design company Geyer Design for execution. The leading hearing aid company Sivantos relocated its global headquarters and its Singapore operations, representing a critical moment to change culture and establish a renewed image and identity. The outcome is a sound-inspired workplace that fosters collaboration, agility, accountability and an entrepreneurial spirit. It is a place that employees are proud of, and that gives visitors a memorable experience.

The facility is intuitively designed, across three very large floor plates, and comprises research & development (R&D), manufacturing, global departments and South East Asia office. Effective spatial planning is integrated into both the visitor and employee flow around the workplace, and it has been developed in an inclusive manner that ensures employees embrace, utilise and understand their new workplace environment.

Connected by Sound

PLH's concept for Sivantos is called "Connected by Sound", whereby the design is a physical manifestation of the experience and connective potential of sound. The workplace design and spatial experience draw on two main themes — "sound unites us" and "sound as a celebration of global diversity". Subsequently, form, light, colour and materiality are integrated to bring visitors and employees together in spaces that are rich in sensory experience.

Upon entering the headquarter, it becomes clear that sound is the focal point of this organization. Inspired by sound waves, an exciting sculptural "sound wall" encases the arrival and reception area — establishing a strong and immediate wow factor to anybody who visits. The visual elements work aesthetically and acoustically to transform sound waves into physical form, and bringing sound to life visually for an emotional and uplifting experience. It is here that global and local visitors want to be photographed with the Sivantos logo as a backdrop. Sivantos Senior Vice President HR, Nicolai R. Jensen, explains how the new headquarters has transformed the working culture at Sivantos.

Evenly Distributed Across Functional Areas

Hubs are centrally located around the floors creating spaces for collaboration, focus, contemplation and break-out. In connection is a series of team support functions such as phone booths, small meeting rooms, cafés, print, storage rooms and various break-out spaces with diverse seating modes that encourage team building, exchange of expert knowledge and collaboration. Easy accessibility and close proximity to all desk areas means all functions are equally distributed through the floors. The hubs act as attractive destinations within the workplace, each with their own sound concept based on the diversity and contrasts of "sound of nature", "sound of the city" and "sound of celebration" creating different "soundscapes" within the office. Each sound is presented in its own unique form and richness in the design of the space, building different emotional scenarios, while returning to the theme of sound.

The names for the collaboration hubs were inspired by the steering committee's ambition statements and core brand values to highlight and celebrate global diversity, invention, and connectivity. The intention was to create different soundscapes within the workspace that would encourage collaboration and create a vibrant and entrepreneurial atmosphere.

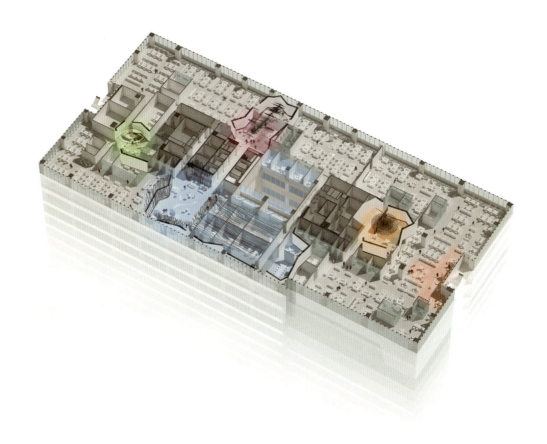

5

COMMERCIAL SPACE

Commercial Space

Open House

Design Agency
Klein Dytham Architecture

Location
Bangkok, Thailand

Area
4,600 m²

Client
Central Embassy Hotel Ltd.

Open House is located in the Central Embassy complex in Bangkok. Within this vast 4,600 m² double-height interior, a village of spaces has been created, each with a familiar human scale — restaurants, lounges, bars, galleries, stores, pop-ups, libraries and workspaces that all seamlessly fit together. A place to hang out, a place to play, a place to catch up on work and a place to eat and drink.

Today's mega cities have turned their back on the people who visit, live and work in them. People are either working, shopping, eating or moving between spaces. There is nowhere to pause, take a breath, sit or simply regain control of your senses, especially in the stifling heat of Bangkok. Open House is seen as an antidote to this — it is an oasis, a getaway. A space where anyone can feel comfortable, at home, spend the day, relax and be inspired.

A Walkabout Layout to Experience the Beauty of Life

The bookstore element, rather than being a large square box, is instead linear and weaves its way through the space — a path with rest spots along the way where you can pause and read. A tall book tower anchors the bookshop at one end of the space, and a large double height library wall wraps around at the other end. The bookstore seamlessly integrates into the bar and restaurant spaces and allows people to browse freely. In a world dominated by online book sales, highly curated bookstores like this, which focus on Asian art and culture, are becoming increasingly important and popular now that the physical browsing experience is everything.

Since opening the space has been a huge success, it is used by locals and tourists alike. "The steps" seating area allows for this kind of activation; the kid's play area is abuzz with noise and fun and there are children-friendly restaurants nearby. Activating the space with talks, book signings, culinary workshops, etc. is key to keeping the space alive and a vital part of the city.

Incorporating Green Ideas

The Central Embassy complex is in a surprisingly leafy area of Bangkok, overlooking the British Embassy complex on one side and greener treetops on the other. The designers wanted to extend this notion of greenery inside and so suggested that the whole of Open House stay under a huge canopy of leaves. To achieve this and reduce the impact of the extensive white ceiling, the designers devised a pattern of leaves that spreads across the whole space. The 9,600 leaves were hand painted over a series of six weeks and collectively create an amazing artwork, an iconic and memorable element of the space.

A co-working space which is located behind the book wall, with green walls, flooring, seating and greenery hanging on shelves, making the space "the greenhouse". The rows of office seating are well organised, provides a quieter, more secluded space for working as well as a suite of meeting rooms. Food and drinks from any one of the restaurants can be ordered and delivered to your desk.

Innovative Tower Design for Seamless Connectivity

Over the last few years Bangkok has become a sophisticated world-class retail and food destination. With the city changing so quickly the challenge was how to design a space that would always be a part of the moment and always be a familiar retreat — a true Open House.

With so many components and functions it became clear right from the outset that navigation was the key to the project. The designers break down this aircraft-like and hanger-like space into an understandable and seamlessly connected village.

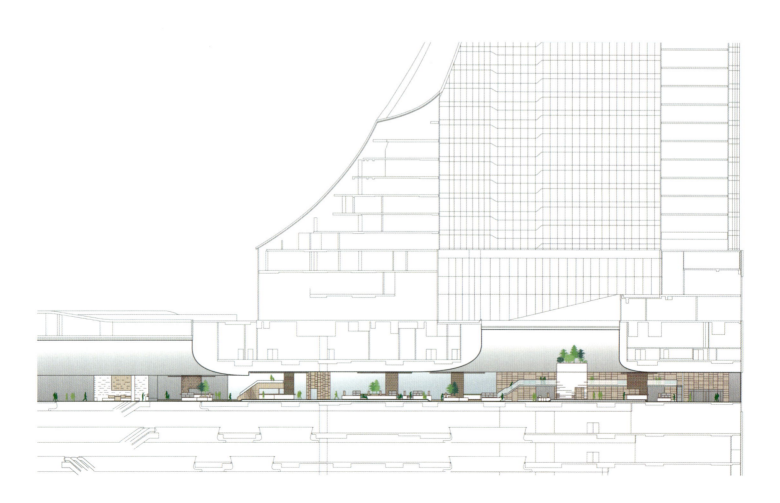

The tower's role in this case speaks for itself: first, make the restaurants visible from a distance by making the towers act like totems; second, hide the kitchen hoods and ventilation ducts; third, enclose many of the columns with the space and reduce their visual impact.

During the day the towers seem more solid while at night they dissolve, creating interesting layering effects and moiré patterns. The towers are clad in a family of different timber fretwork patterns; the variety in these patterns serves to change the way light passes through the towers as you move through the space. Mirrored panels on the ceiling around the towers make them appear to extend beyond the space and also break down the immensity of the ceiling.

Commercial Space

Molecure Pharmacy

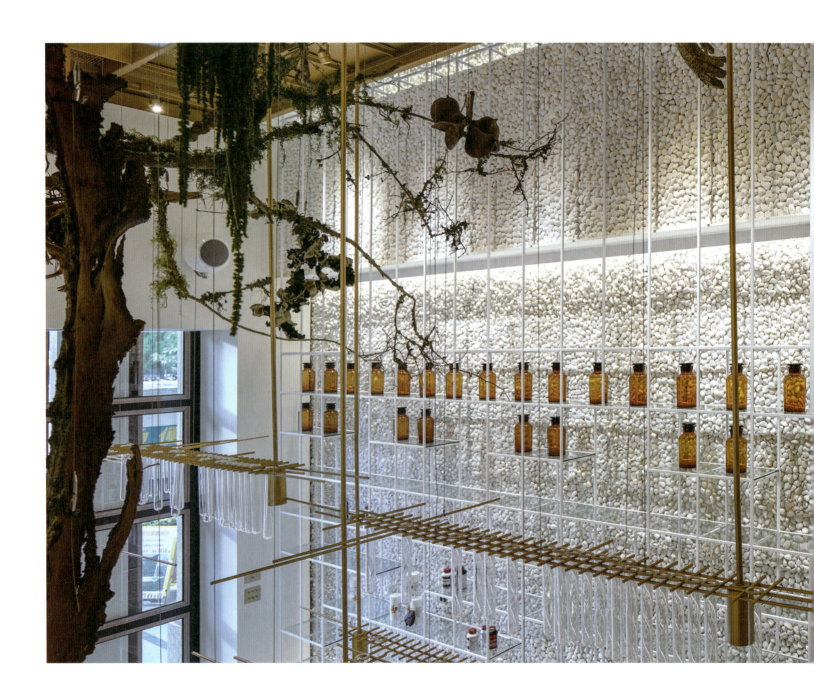

Design Agency
Waterfrom Design

Location
Taiwan, China

Area
120 m²

Photographer
Guomin Li

The owner of this project is a post 80s from a pharmacy family, as the third generation, he hopes to subvert the traditional image of pharmacy, bring the three-generations traditional pharmacy a totally different look and melt it into the diversified modern environment. It also brings people who pay increasing attention to health a new space which integrates function, aesthetics, and experimental spirit.

Geometric Figures Mimicking Molecular Aggregation

Like MOLECURE is split and reorganized from words "Molecule" and "Cure", while approaching to the design, designer returns to the original purpose of pharmacy — extracting molecule from nature to synthesize healing drugs. Thus, designers get the idea of building a space which they named "green in the lab", combining the seemingly conflicting qualities of "primitive" with "technology", just like new compounds formed due to molecular bombardment.

Ways of molecular aggregation varies from triangular to polygonal, spherical to cones, and the change on its shape due to different ways of aggregation could be amazing. We extracted the two characteristics of molecule — "connectivity" and "aggregation" into our design. For example, we used cement to stick cobblestones on the two towering walls on the left and right side, whose rough texture gives people a sense of being real. The metal, lightweight glass and transparent acrylics are crisscrossing, and straight lines are adopted to build the display racks which is in longitude-and-latitude shape; just as repeated expanding of the molecule — with drugs put on them, the display racks seem to disappear from the space, while the colourful drugs act as paintings to colour the walls. The space is thus floating with breath-taking abstract art atmosphere.

An Innovative Customer Experience

One-way mode of traditional pharmacy counter service is avoided here, the core of the space is a laboratory table, where pharmacists interact with customers. Together with the open dispensing area, and iPad embedded consulting service system, interactive information aggregation function and innovative customer experience are created. The laboratory table is stacked with solid wood, original cortex of a trunk over a hundred year is taken as the base of the table, together with the hanging green plants that grow profusely, and it looks like an original forest. These designs subvert the dumb atmosphere of a traditional pharmacy, and also turn medicine and health care into a healthier lifestyle.

As an unprecedented integration of three business types — drug display, dispensing experiments, and life experience, what connects them is a curvy copper corkscrew staircase, which makes people think of DNA double spiral structure in molecular biology. Countless molecule-like triangular holes are cut by laser on the stairs to create shadows which symbols scattered shadow of leaves. This acts as a salute to the nature.

Just as the owner desired, Molecule Pharmacy not only gets rid of the fixed stereotype of Pharmacies but also improves the value of existence of Taiwan's stagnant pharmacy industry.

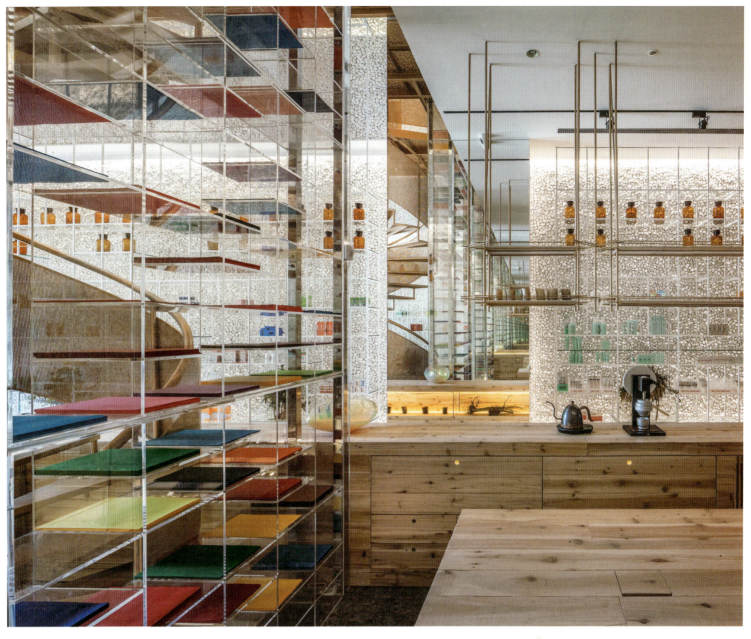

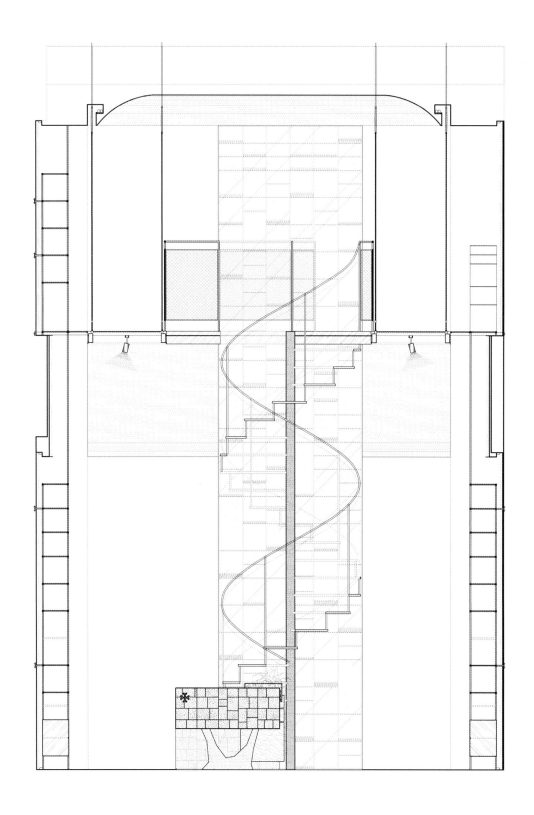

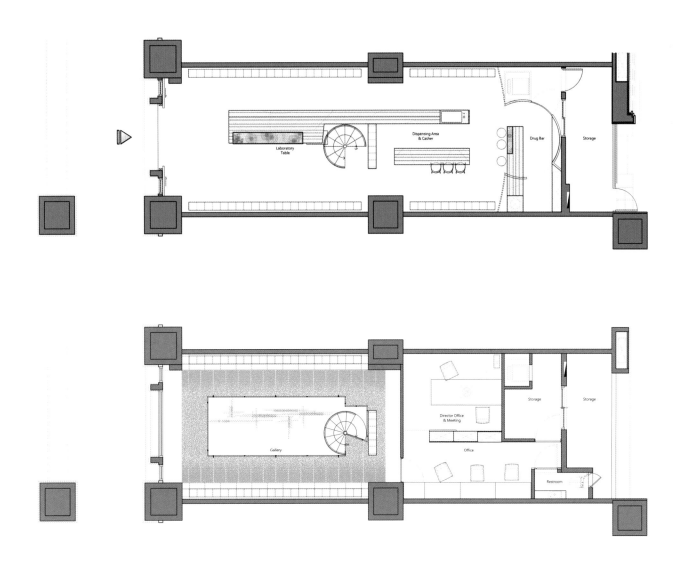
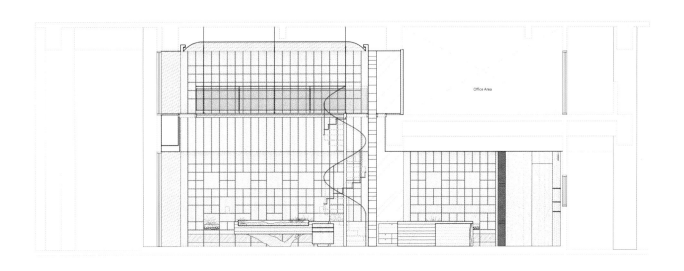

Commercial Space

Cor Shop

Design Agency
BLOCO Arquitetos

Location
Brasilia, Brazil

Area
180 m²

Photography
Haruo Mikami

The COR shop is located in the underground parking of a shopping mall in Brasília, Brazil. The client's briefing for the shop "COR" (colour in Portuguese) asked designers to create a space that could work both as a showroom for a brazilian brand of paintings and architectural coatings and as the backdrop for the display of the work of the furniture designer Paulo Alves, from São Paulo. At the same time the space should be flexible enough to host parties and events.

Play a Little Game with Colours

The designers created a series of white walls that serve mainly as a background for the furniture. These walls were positioned in space according to a single point of perspective at the main entrance of the shop. Therefore, from that specific point of view, the showroom looks like a sequence of white walls, floor and ceiling. This specific point of observation is marked by a white circle on the floor inside the black room that precedes the entrance. Let the customers feel the colours and the little games they do.

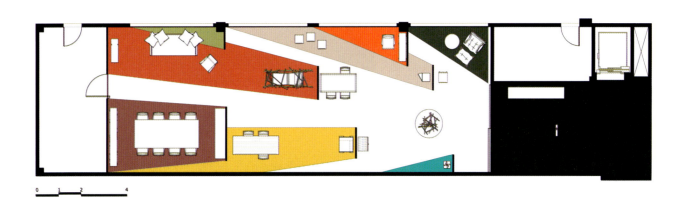

However, small "pockets" of colourful walls, floors and ceilings are revealed as one enters the shop. This was achieved following the lines of perspective from the defined point of view to define the limits of the colour surfaces. The internal colours are only revealed through the movement of the visitor. A secondary display window faces small group of parking spaces. Only from this point of view it is possible to see the whole internal space at once.

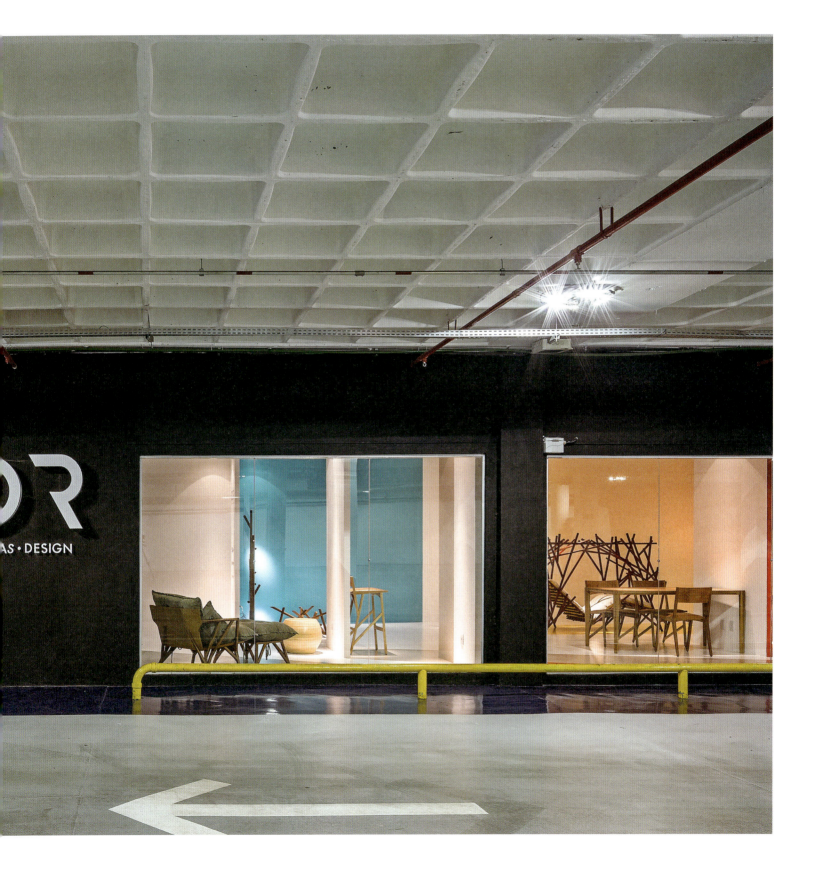

The Design of a Commercial Space Should Start with the Object Itself on Display

For the two requirements mentioned above, the design team needed to achieve such a big differentiation in a limited space at the same time. They looked at the work of Paulo Alves as a starting point. They saw his love for the concrete art as an element that could connect all the proposed uses: colour.

According to Theo Van Doesburg in his Concrete Art manifesto from 1930, "Concretism is not abstract because nothing is more concrete and real than the line, the colour and the surface". In this case designers were interested in transforming the abstract notion of colour into something palpable in space. Therefore, their looked at the work of artists such as Felix varini and George Rousse and their aim of creating forms that only exist when observed from a specific point of view.

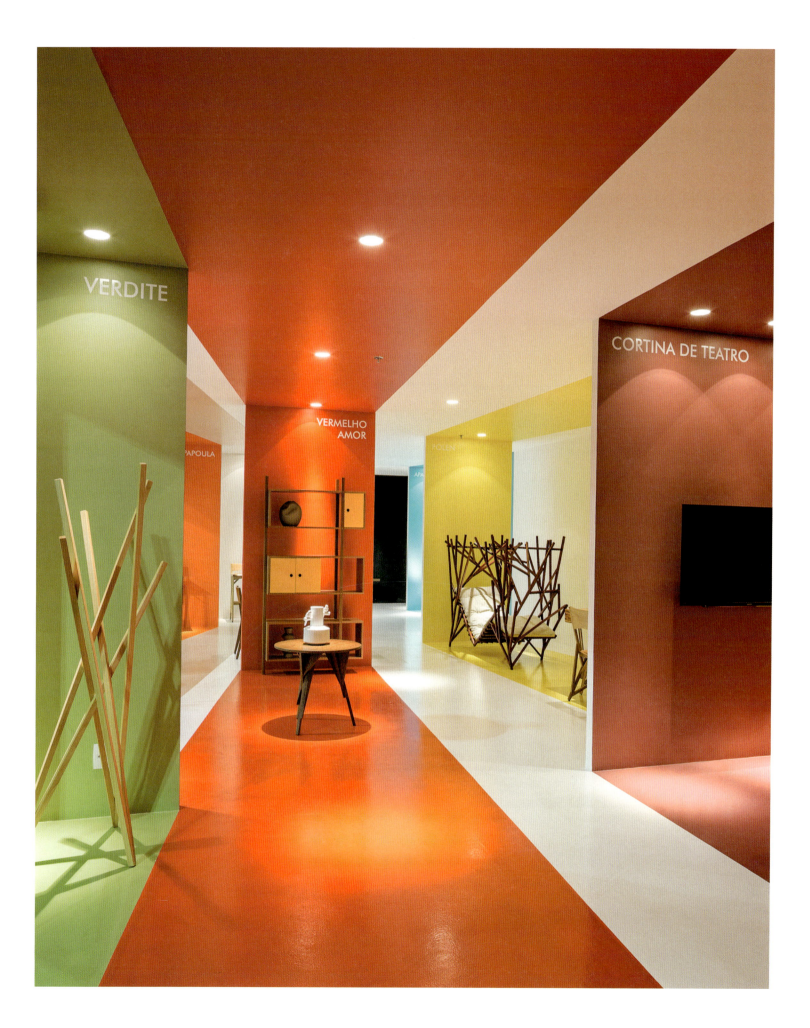

Commercial Space

Galeries Lafayette Flagship On Champs-Élysées

Design Agency
BIG-Bjarke Ingels Group

Area
6,800 m²

Location
Paris, France

Client
Groupe Galeries Lafayette

Located on the iconic Avenue des Champs-Élysées, the historic Art Deco bank building from 1932 is uncovered and celebrated to create a carefully curated retail laboratory for world's leading fashion, food and lifestyle brands to come together with each other and the surrounding city. The 6,800 m² Galeries Lafayette concept store officially opened its doors to the public in March 2019. The generous four-story environment is the largest store on the famed Parisian boulevard and combines old world elegance with modern chic, hosting established and emerging brands, experiences and events.

A Blend of Old and New Textures

Design pays tribute to the tactility and texture of the historical building. Throughout the store, visitors encounter precious materials and refined details from the past that are reinterpreted and deployed in a contemporary way. Walking around the lofty gallery-like space feels as moving through a composition of architectural elements that operate at the scale of furniture and create defined experiential shopping zones.

Shoppers are invited into the building through an inverse canopy on the street level. A glowing bridge ushers life into the heart of the building: a dramatic circular atrium covered by a monumental glass cupola that has been restored and uncovered for maximum daylight.

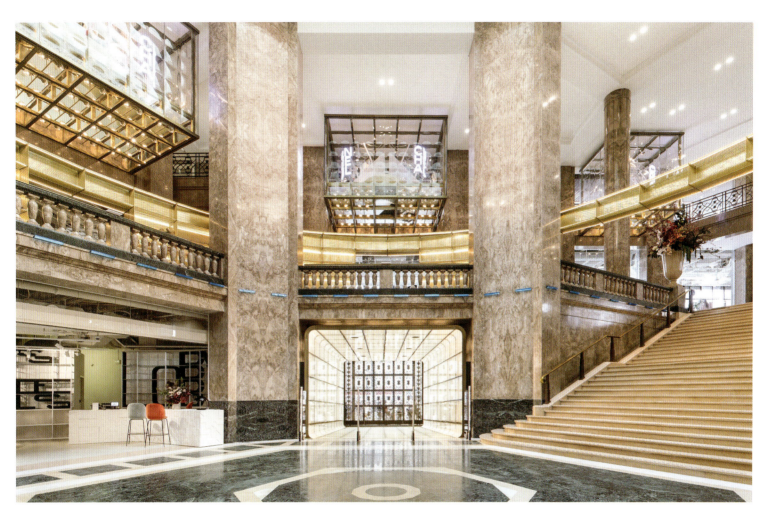

Exciting Floors

The entire store unfolds itself on the ground floor and creates a bright new urban living room for brand activations, fashion shows and other special events. A grand staircase can double as an auditorium during events. From the ground floor, visitors are immediately able to see the upper levels enticing them to explore the different destinations and activities. The top floor features a series of suspended glass vitrines that look like independent objects and can host a variety of experiences and activities visible from the lower levels.

Customers enter the first floor via the stairs. It features creative and emerging brands, as well as a denim lab, jewellery display, limited edition sneakers and tech products. A continuous golden ring of perforated metal wraps around all of the columns and creates a series of rooms and alcoves facing the atrium.

The escalators are finished in warm metal and a ribbon of glass in the same material palette as the central atrium. Exploring the store and its different levels feels like a carefully curated environment where furniture is never only storage: interweaving carpets become dressing rooms, countertops are a sculptural stack of elements, magic carpets for the shoe display double as furniture for the shoppers to sit and try the footwear.

On the second floor, shoppers can dine in the Oursin restaurant while enjoying views of the city or relax at the Citron coffee lounge on the first floor, both designed by French fashion designer Simon Porte Jacquemus and operated by Caviar Kaspia. Meanwhile, the entire basement floor is a Parisian food court, where groceries and eateries are divided into sweet and savoury sections and where massive counters are arranged around welcoming shared tables.

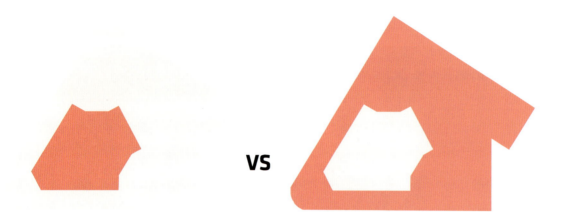

The Heart VS. The Periphery

The heart of the building pays tribute to the tactility and texture of the historical building. The historical architecture is supplemented by the raw, gallery-like periphery with high ceilings and abundance daylight.

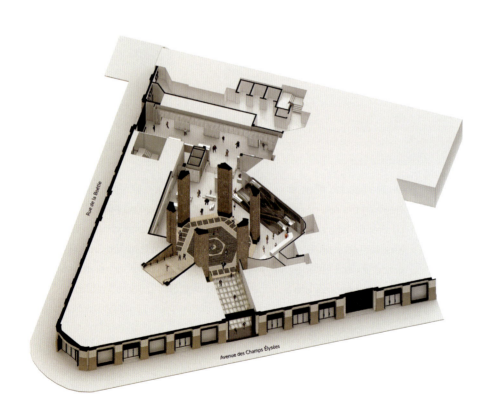

Commercial Space

Shiseido

Design Agency
Nendo

Location
Tokyo, Japan

Area
430 m²

Photography
At the Courtesy of Nendo

Shiseido, started in 1872, is the largest cosmetics company in Japan. This project, designed by Nendo, is Japan's first Western-style pharmacy in Ginza, Tokyo. It has four floors, each serving various functions and services. Cosmetics are sold on the ground and first floors: products on the ground floor are aimed at foreign tourists, and the first floor also houses a skin care salon. There is a photo studio and a hair and make-up salon on the second floor and on the third floor there is a cafe, event space and private booths for beauty consultations.

Similarities Between Interior Design and Make-Up

The main concept of the interior design was to integrate the common elements of interior construction and make-up. When preparing a wall or floor, first you apply the undercoat, then layers of paint or buffing, and finally a protective topcoat. Make-up follows a similar order. Skin care products are first applied, then primed with primer and foundation, followed by a dab of colour, such as lipstick or eye shadow. The similarities in these processes inspired the concept of the refurbished space, where make-up is applied in the interior of the shop using Shiseido products and related materials.

Paper made from thinly spread cotton pads was used on the walls; lit from underneath, it gives off a soft glow. Camellia oil — a key ingredient at Shiseido, especially in its hair care products — was applied to natural, unprocessed wood, to give it a beautiful aged finish as time passes.

Eye shadow was layered onto the walls with make-up brushes to give a marble-like finish, and nail polish was mixed into the paint used for the ceiling art, giving a subtle shimmer that catches the shifting light. Hidden touches like these have their roots in the Japanese sense of beauty and are a fitting expression of Shiseido's perspective.

Brand Logo is the Best Visual Symbol

The forms of the theme, each inspired by techniques from Japan's traditional crafts, can be found throughout the space: it appears in the form of columns, resembling sections of bamboo; as cut-outs in the style of kiri-e paper craft; in woven patterns resembling traditional baskets; and modelled like traditional papier-mâché hariko.

Finally, string curtains were used behind the windows of the building. A traditional decorative knot called awajimusubi, was tied at specific points on the strings to form the outline of a camellia flower when viewed from afar. The awajimusubi knot is a traditional Japanese symbol which stands for a long-lasting bond and connection, representing Shiseido's desire to build an enduring relationship with its customers.

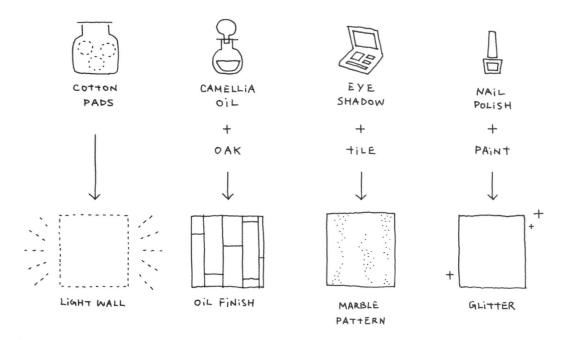

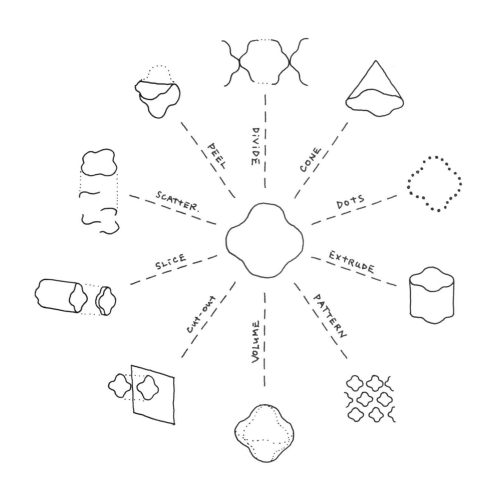

Commercial Space

Delvaux "le 27" In Brussels

Design Agency
Vudafieri-Saverino Partners

Location
Brussels, Belgium

Area
270 m²

Photography
Santi Caleca

Delvaux, the oldest luxury leather goods house in the world, founded in Belgium in 1829, has inaugurated a new store in the heart of Brussels: "Le 27". It is housed in a majestic Mansion on Boulevard de Waterloo, a high-end luxury shopping area.

The project is signed by the studio Vudafieri-Saverino, which since 2012 has been responsible for the design of Delvaux stores worldwide (more than 40 of them, including boutiques in Paris, London, Shanghai, Tokyo, Dubai...), creating boutiques that are always different from one other.

Set out on two floors, the store has retained its original structure. Four-metre-high ceilings give a broader scope and brightness to an environment where materials such as marble, wood and wrought iron stand out. The grand staircase at the entrance leads to the spacious upper floor which is immersed in surreal light projected through the windows of the Art Deco skylight.

Combine the Display Cases in Geometry Module

Through a refined interaction of modular elements that combine geometric rigour and trompe-l'oeil supports, the display fittings organise, rationalise and embellish the presentation of bags and accessories. Designed as a combination of minimal asymmetrical shapes, they are enriched by the use of precious materials commonly used in furniture design during the art-deco period, such as marble or polished nickel. Geometric and classical form is balanced by vertical light-grey coloured bands, which interrupt the symmetry.

The combination of the apparently "poor" material and finishes of the Mondrian-style wall displays, the richly baroque finish of the wardrobes and the out-centred coloured stripes, disrespectful of classical spaces, creates a balanced cohabitation between classic and modern, order and disorder, rule, and exception. A contrast that reflects the Delvaux attitude that presents rigorously classic forms, dialectically combined with extremely modern, chic, slightly playful additions.

A Small Furniture Museum as Well as a Showroom

The furnishings are enriched by emblematic Belgian design pieces created by the greatest designers of the twentieth century: Jules Wabbes, Pieter de Bruyne, Renaat Braem, Emiel Verannema. All works signed in limited editions, unique and rare, worthy of a museum collection.

There is also room for pieces by contemporary Belgian designers (Nathalie Dewez, Alain Berteau and Ben Storms) and international designers, such as the Italian Gino Sarfatti, master of lighting design. The globular shapes recall those of the Atomium, Belgium's iconic pavilion at the 1958 World Fair in Brussels.

A Dialogue with Art

Between the ground and the first floor what appears to be a collection of ancient paintings turns out to be a series of photographs, archival pigment prints by the Argentine artist Romina Ressia in which her post-neo-Flemish portraits are combined with daily and kitsch artefacts, yet another brilliant twist and playful illusion.

A collection of twentieth-century Belgian ceramics appears here and there on a wall, stacked high, embodying the fantastic, endless creativity of Belgian artists. The richness of the colours also echoes the Delvaux leather products in the showroom.

In "Le 27" the Maison's bags and accessories meet works of art and design that turn the boutique into a museum in constant evolution, a genuine place of encounter, dialogue and discovery. Open to visitors, ideal for wandering around with its historical, contemporary and eclectic furnishings destined to change as new pieces are acquired, "Le 27" is a deliberately original and decidedly unique environment. So unique that it will not be reproduced, ever, anywhere in the world.

6

FOOD SPACE

Food Space

Fish On Fire

Design Agency
YOD Design Lab

Location
Odessa, Ukraine

Area
432 m²

Photography
Roman Kupriyan

Fish on Fire (Pesce al Forno) is an Italian fish restaurant of known restaurateur Savelii Libkin. It is opened in the heart of Odessa on the corner of the street Derybasivska, which is a calling card of the city. The name of the institution primarily reflects its general concept. Into this concept is laid both a way of cooking on fire in the furnace and that the materials used in the decoration had undergone heat treatment too.

Dine in the "Depths of the Sea"

Since the restaurant specializes in fish dishes, in creating the interior of the restaurant designers tried to portray the marine theme through a series of associations, such as the floor which is covered with a heat-treated ash tree, and walls which are burnt with different gradient copper squama. Ropes that cover the entire ceiling were used previously by sailors, highlighting the age and vicissitudes of the material.

According to the concept, the basement is "submerged" by water so the whole restaurant is like "woven" from fishnet. The ceiling resembles the surface of the seabed with craters of underwater geysers, from which hang the round glass lamps. Specially developed by the studio fixtures with a caustic effect create the impression of glimmer of light in the thicker of seawater what amplify the "underwater" stay. Given that here is a bar and one more restaurant hall, the caustic effect on the walls and fixtures in the form of large oblong bubbles create here more "evening" and chamber atmosphere.

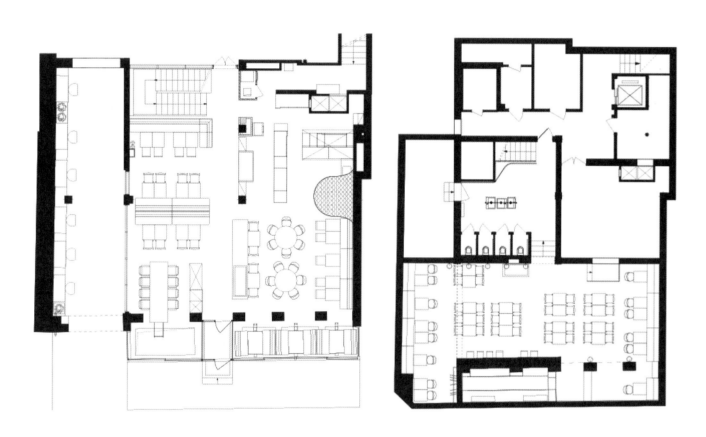

Food Space

Gaga King Glory

Design Agency
COORDINATION ASIA

Location
Guangdong, China

Area
525 m²

Photography
COORDINATION ASIA

With the theme of "presenting an enjoyable and vibrant lifestyle", Gaga King Glory provides a breezy and light oasis of calm in the busy city for a young, trendy and sophisticated demographic of Chinese consumers, bringing a green and quality living experience to the urban population. This project is located in Shenzhen, Guangdong, one of the most prosperous metropolises in the country. It is imagined as both an oasis for shoppers, as well as an inspiring setting for meeting with friends, catching up on emails, or simply relaxing.

Blurring the Boundaries Between Inside and Outside

Gaga King Glory's expansive entrance and floor-to- ceiling glass facade draws visitors into the space. With attractive outdoor seating for some 64 diners, as well as tables extending into the mall itself, the design blurs the boundaries between inside and outside, establishing the venue's relaxed, informal atmosphere from the outset.

Designed with versatility in mind, they include a central raised lounge area: flanked by low-level tables, plush banquette seating and contemporary chairs, it also features high tables and stools. Moving closer towards the cornflower-blue counter, eye-catching cylindrical benches offer a more informal spot for those grabbing a quick coffee on the go. These unique zoning areas create a relaxed and casual atmosphere for the entire shopping street. For cosy catch ups, two additional lounge areas see comfy sofas and statement lighting create a home-from-home for respite and relaxation; while long communal tables are ideal for groups, be they drinking, eating, or working.

Idyllic Beach Atmosphere

Conceived as an idyllic beach — just a short distance from Shenzhen's industrious port — this newest venue maintains the brand's reputation for stylish design, exceptional coffee, and above all, as a place to inspire. Each with their own unique ambience and feel, spaces are distinguished through furniture styles and lighting types. Inside, the 400 m² interior appears as an ocean of blues, turquoises, and greens. A colour palette of midnight blue, teal blue, and aquamarine, it evokes the tranquillity of an idyllic beach in the heart of one of China's most buzzing metropolises!

Connecting both Gaga's interior and exterior elements is a lamella ceiling in bright white aluminum. Reminiscent of a crashing wave, it signals a subtle beach theme that runs throughout the design, while its dramatic curves hint at the flexibility of the wider venue. The combination of terrazzo and wooden flooring is reminiscent of a sandy beach, with the combination of the two tones bringing the warmth and softness of walking barefoot on the beach. Throughout, pendent lighting in burnished bronze and black lend an intimacy to the space, while adjustable LED lights concealed inside the lamella ceiling carry the eatery through day, to dusk, and night.

Large potted cacti deliver welcome pops of colour and texture throughout the space, while geometric terrariums of succulents make for eye-catching table top details. Wall decorations — including circular mirrors, curved neon lights, and disc-shaped artworks — complement the arched lamella overhead, providing Gaga's digitally savvy clientele with an eminently shareable, social media-friendly backdrop.

Food Space

Cocina Hermanos Torres Restaurant

Design Agency
Office of Architecture in Barcelona: OAB

Location
Barcelona, Spain

Area
800 m²

Photography
Joan Guillamat

Over time the space of the kitchen has gradually acquired a certain protagonist in some of the more recent avant-garde restaurants. To begin with, picture windows were put in which showed the interior of the kitchen, behind glass at first. On other occasions the kitchen was opened by placing it at the far end of the premises behind a bar, and in some cases, one even acceded to the restaurant via the kitchen. In some restaurants, too, exclusive tables have been included so that a few clients could dine inside the kitchen itself.

Cocina Hermanos Torres is a new space, one that is ideal for living a new culinary experience. Container and content come together in the interests of a unique experience.

"More Than A Restaurant with A Kitchen We'd Like to Create A Kitchen with A Restaurant"

Right from the start Sergio and Javier Torres defined what they were after in a few words: "More than a restaurant with a kitchen we'd like to create a kitchen with a restaurant." With this clear and ambitious premise in mind and with the acquisition on their part of a former industrial shed of almost 800 m², which it was necessary to completely overhaul, the project could begin.

At the spatial level the project is created with a view to effacing or blurring a few dividing lines between the different spaces that make up a traditional restaurant. This time, however, an even more radical step has been taken by locating the kitchen as not only the central feature of the intervention but also as an immersive element. The restaurant is the kitchen.

In situating the kitchen in the epicentre of the restaurant the old concept is resurrected of the café-theatre, places where diners enjoy a show while they eat. Diners participate and empathize with the Chef and are the eye-witnesses of the creative act that is unfolding. And not only are they the eye-witnesses, they also end up becoming the main protagonists of the experience when the dish is set before them on the table.

A space of no more than two meters, devoid of all physical or visual obstacles. This is what the brothers were seeking — to be able to establish a direct rapport with their clients. Added to which, thanks to having chosen an industrial shed as a great container, the experience diners have of personally living through a "performance" is emphasized. Being in such a huge shed is like being present in a television studio or a modern theatre.

Novel Layout Design for More Efficient Food Preparation

In three of the sides which wrap around the central space there are the bodega, patisserie, and the three kitchens where the food is prepared (Meat, Fish, and Fruit&Vegetables), as well as the research and development space where the brothers undertake their experiments and tests for inventing new creations, which can be observed behind glass.

Much work has been done so that the kitchens function like clockwork, and they are as ideally equipped as possible. On account of this, there is a circulation space to the rear which manages to connect all the spaces together: the kitchens for preparation and production and their respective annexes as well as spaces for the personnel, canteen, cloakrooms, training room, etc. Not with standing the novel nature of the layout, then, the space has been organized in a coherent and efficient manner.

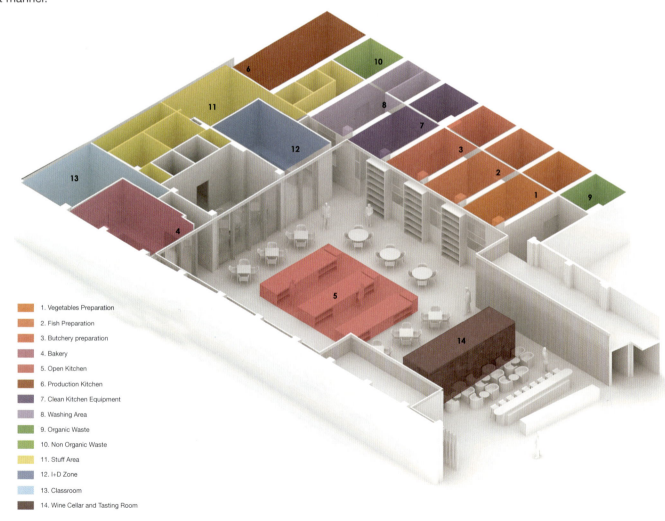

1. Vegetables Preparation
2. Fish Preparation
3. Butchery preparation
4. Bakery
5. Open Kitchen
6. Production Kitchen
7. Clean Kitchen Equipment
8. Washing Area
9. Organic Waste
10. Non Organic Waste
11. Stuff Area
12. I+D Zone
13. Classroom
14. Wine Cellar and Tasting Room

A Little Pre-Dinner Surprise

Another example would be that of respecting the classical concept of a lobby or atrium represented in the area of the Bar. In other words, when customers enter and accede to the big industrial shed, they have a first filter-like space available to them that enables them to hold back the surprise of the subsequent discovery of the ample space of the main dining room.

The Bar is turned into a lobby, reverting to the concept of a foyer in a concert hall: before the show the barman, a renowned mixologist, will prepare us a cocktail, a first aperitif, which introduces us to the atmosphere of the shed, the perfect curtain-raiser before the experience which awaits us on the other side of the bodega.

Simplify and Only Allow the Truly Important to Dominate

Once the organization of the space has been defined, an element of great importance comes into play for ensuring that the culinary experience occurs with the degree of comfort and convenience that it merits. In order to stress the undeniable fact that we are dining in an industrial shed a series of materials are introduced, which tone down the space and even manage to produce a sort of ambiguity between being, initially, in a cold space of huge proportions as opposed to an agreeable, warm and welcoming space.

The tables with tablecloths, the cushioned seats, and even the presence of the occasional carpet will temper things and provide comfort as well as help to control the acoustics of the room.

Having said that, an attempt has been made to ensure that the decorative interventions are as minimal as possible. Designers eschewed the recent and increasingly tiring fashion for overloading spaces with objects, fabrics and a formal abundance that gives rise to a baroque or neo-kitsch minimalism that only confuses the client and makes it unclear what is authentic and what is fake. Of doing away with the unnecessary, of not confusing things.

Food Space

Sintoho Restaurant At The Four Seasons Hotel

Design Agency
Kokaistudios

Location
Kuwait

Area
500 m²

Photography
Seth Powers

The Sintoho restaurant is named after the combination of Singapore, Tokyo and Hong Kong. This project located on the top floor of the newly built Four Seasons Kuwait in the Burj Alshaya building. Having previously worked together on the Brasserie at the Four Seasons Kyoto, they are working together for the second time.

Kuwait has a shortage of fine dining restaurants serving quality Asian cuisine, so the hotel invited Kokaistudios to conceive an innovative F&B destination that could elevate the street foods of the cities of Singapore, Tokyo and Hong Kong into a fine dining destination and experience.

Designer set about creating a temple to Asian cuisine and craftsmanship that eschewed kitschy and thematic styles and aimed for the creation of an essential and refreshing space in which the dining experience is influenced both by the architecture of the space and the food offering.

Identifying Commonalities from Different Cultures

The restaurant design was conceived first and foremost around the idea of celebrating the diversity and excellence of Asian cuisine and creating spaces and opportunities for the guests to experience the sights, smells and tastes of these food cultures up close.

Designers searched for commonalities between the cultures in order to come up with a design language to unite them and they took their inspiration less from the current nature of the individual countries but rather from the historical role that Chinese culture has played over time throughout Asia and how those influences continue to be part of everyday life.

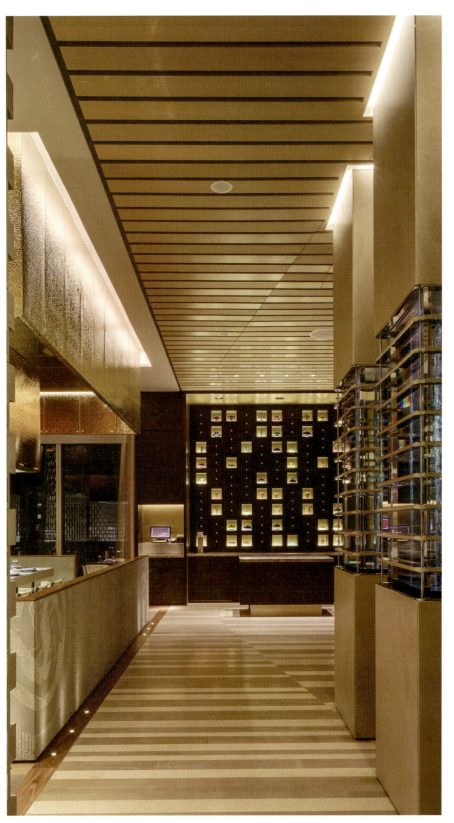

Integrating Historic Craftsmanship into the Space

The entrance area of the restaurant features a long corridor flanked on one side by an expansive green wall filled primarily with local desert plant and on the other by a series of custom designed water towers which combine to create a cooling and soothing experience. The corridor finishes in a tea wall fronted by an elaborate carved wood tea station where guests can select an expansive choice of fine teas. To the right of the entrance corridor sits the main open dining area on the right that features expansive 12 m high ceilings that offers expansive views of the city and the Persian Gulf beyond.

The sushi bar in the dining area is made from traditional Japanese burnt cedar boards. The wood has been specially treated to become black and shiny like lacquer after burning in a hot fire. The hand-laid brass trim and wooden scorched marks add to the atmosphere and sophistication of the sushi bar. The soft lighting in the area comes from the series of water drop glass pendants produced by the London based artisans DHLiberty Lux.

The rest of the public area seating is cantered largely around the individual open live cooking stations where guests can take a close look at the preparation of robatta, teppanyaki, and dim sum and other delicacies from Hong Kong which have been clad by hand-hammered metal hoods and sculpted stone bases featuring images and motifs typical inspired by classical designs found in China. The floral pattern on the wall undulating form appears as a dynamic wave while being in actuality a straight structure.

The strong inter-play between the main materials of wood, stone, and hand-finished metals is thrown a curve by the insertion of a 3D feature wall made of exposed concrete forms that runs the length of the kitchen wall.

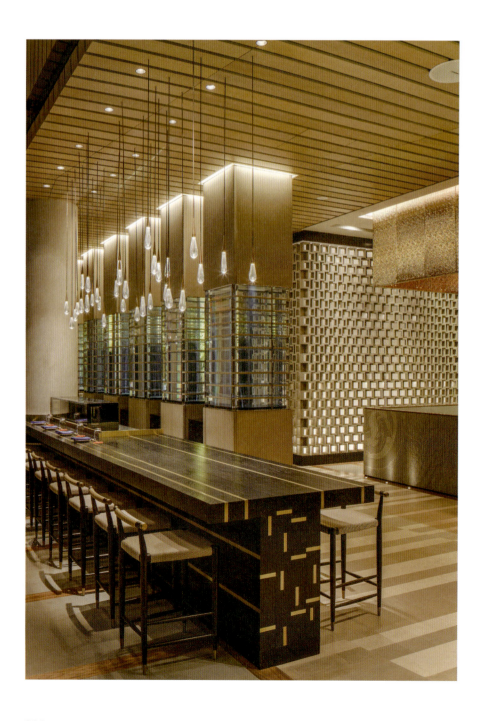

Combination of East and West Makes the Space Glamorous

The private dining rooms are an ode to Chinese embroidery craftsmanship with bespoke chairs and walls featuring hand-printed linen fabric albeit with a wink to Venice via the use of the Fortuny silk pendant lamps and red Murano glass inlays.

For bathrooms, designers cooperated with a Shanghai based video production team Flatmind to create a series of Chinese shadow video installations that are projected on the grey hand hammered Chinese stone.

A strong architectural approach to the design of interiors with an original use of materials and light to create unexpected subtle emphatic feeling between the space and the people; handcrafted materials shaped and controlled up to the finest detail interact and interplay with both the day and night light and reveal an incredibly expressive power.

Food Space

Wood Mountain—Anti-domino No. 02

Design Agency
Daipu Architects

Location:
Chongqing, China

Area:
120 m²

Photography
Wu Qingshan

Wood Mountain is a bar located in Chongqing, China. It was the first work to be completed in Daipu Architects "Anti-Domino" series. In recent years, our studio has been working on a series of renovation projects. This is a legacy phenomenon caused by the mass and fast production during the past 10-20 years in the construction industry, and it impels us to proactively reflect on and respond to the professional reality behind this phenomenon.

All of these renovation projects can be seen as simple replications of the Domino system in the horizontal dimension and repeated compositions of such system in the vertical dimension. A word, a sentence, or even a piece of manifesto, does not become proper or rational even if it has been repeated thousands of times.

That is why the design agency makes different attempts in each renovation project to respond to these existing and constantly repeated "errors" and "lack of quality", experiment with more enriched and more prototype-driven solutions to renew the existing structure, and expects to generate completely new building systems and structural systems.

Bringing out the Best in Mountain Features

Chongqing, is known as the "City of Mountains" due to its fantastical topography and is also known as the "4D City". People who arrive in Chongqing for the first time will feel excited when they see such distinctive geospatial features. However, it is regrettable to see all the new buildings in this city (including commercial, residential, urban complexes etc.) are the same type as the buildings in all other Chinese first-tier cities. The architectural forms do not respond to and respect the local topography, landscape and climate.

How to create a response to integrate the outdoor environment (including the distant view of Yangtze River) with such a concrete structure within only two column spans and less than 100 m²? This is the primary question designers consider. It also includes the reason why the owner chooses this site for his pub, he wants to have all the people who like beer in Chongqing come here to enjoy the pleasing environment, as well as the nice and unique skyline of the Yuzhong peninsula from both indoor and outdoor perspectives.

So the designers employ a set of new structural language in this project, to simulate the special mountainous space of Chongqing. The mountainous terrain is introduced into the restricted concrete space with integration of a more subtle scale of furniture.

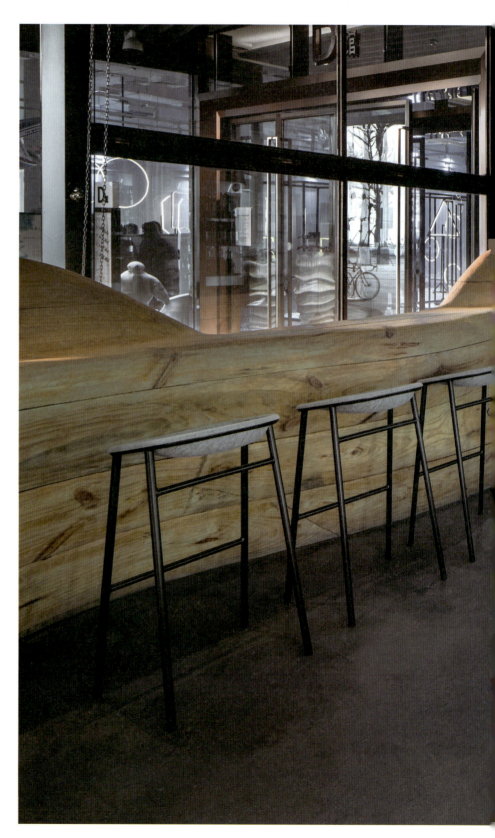

The guide of sight line at the entrance, spatial partitions, footrests of bar counter, small articles for stroking while drinking, and large wood sofa and so on. The whole model is made of pure solid wood and carved by computerized digital control machine. The model is designed on computer, then prefabricated in the factory and assembled on site. This technique improves the completeness of the model and also saves the time of on-site work.

The solid wood will partly expand or contract with the effect of the local wet weather, and varied wood grains will emerge on the surface. Designers expect it will dehisce after one or two years and show a more natural effect of wood piling, just like the appealing scene in a warehouse of timber mill. People will also leave the signs of frequent use on the surface, which seems to implicitly suggest the changes of fermented beer in the barrel.

  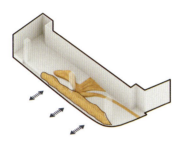

The "Anti-Domino" Series Rethinks the Meaning of Architecture

This project also provides a chance for us to rethink the mega-structure such as super high-rise. As a critical reflection toward the Domino system, designers find that the existing super high-rise design is only a repeated stack of the single layer structure, allowing limited connection between the layers. Moreover, the super high-rise is not only a closed structure inside, but also a lonely island in the city. It is like Narcissis who only has self-worship, and refuses the possibility of any interaction.

The designers use such a new topographical structure to replace the previous horizontal floor, and a completely new public space will be generated inside the super high-rise. It creates connection through the roof garden, top-level residential blocks, work units on the middle floors, and the commercial space on the ground floor. The efficiency of high-rise co-exists with the comfort of lower level, and landmark and openness reach a settlement.

The designer amplifies the dimensional feeling of the space, and also introduces the more relaxed body gestures (sit, lie, squat, lean) of the Chongqing local people (as well as how a natural person in an old neighbourhood will behave) into such a scene of modern life.

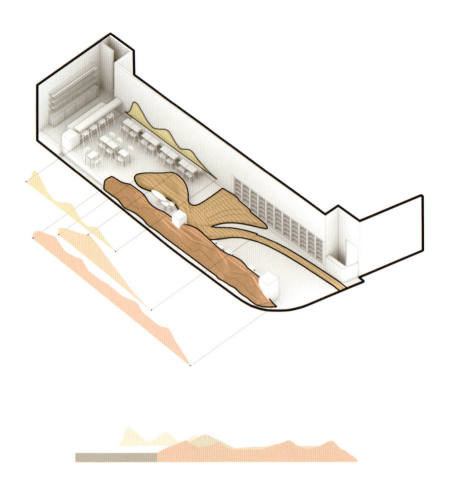

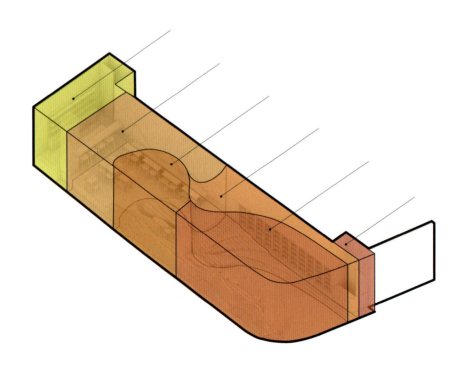

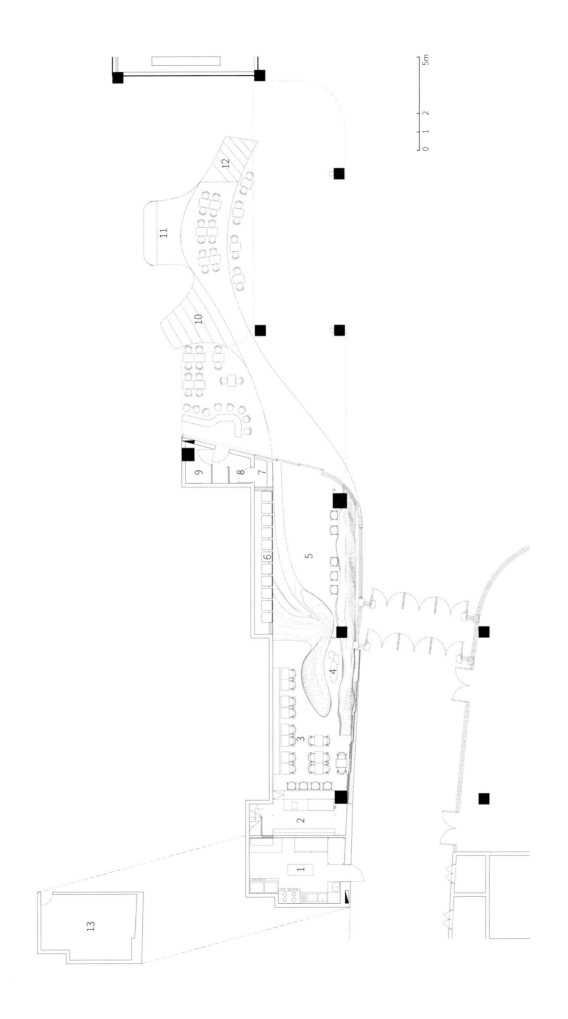

7

EXHIBITION SPACE

Exhibition Space

The Culinary Village: Arda Showroom

Design Agency
LUKSTUDIO

Location
Zhejiang, China

Area
1,000 m²

Photography
Peter Dixie

Based on the idea that a kitchen is the heart of a home, Lukstudio creates a culinary village where kitchen appliances are displayed in four domestic settings, alongside a gallery, a cooking classroom, a VIP lounge, and a multi-functional courtyard. The design has transformed the original 1000 m² mechanical floor into a complete brand experience for manufacturer Arda.

Reinventing the experience of a conventional kitchen showroom, Lukstudio has created an artificial village of different homes, set in a cozy courtyard that brings water, daylight and plants into close proximity. While the project presents many possible consumer experiences, it also reflects on the essence of an ideal living environment.

Ideal Living Environment

Situated by a reflective pool and framed by green walls, a white box marks the entrance of the journey. Following stepping stones in the shallow water, visitors enter a dark tunnel. On the left, an introductory video is accompanied by a water feature of dishwasher jets; on the right, a peek into the courtyard ahead of their discovery.

The main display area is organized as a series of white huts, each presenting an ideal kitchen: minimalistic white, total black, rustic country and modern American. Lukstudio has placed these volumes carefully, carving out strategic openings to create a visual dialogue with one's movement.

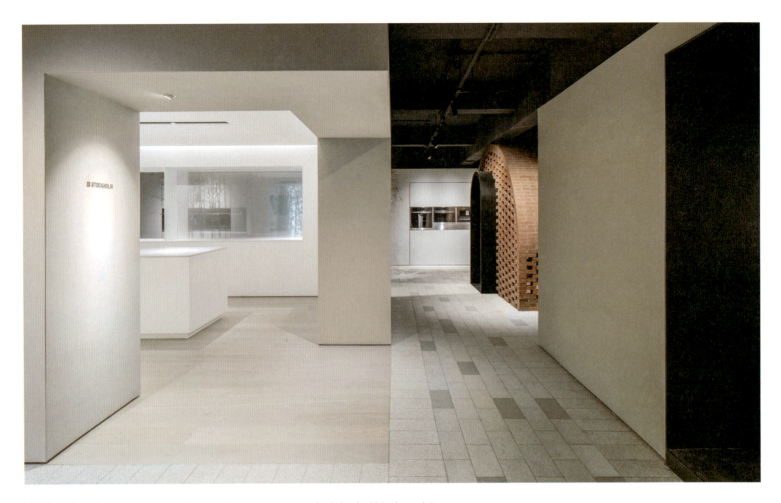

Walking along the stone pavement, one will come upon a vaulted shed within the quiet "village". Reminiscent of an outdoor kiln, the space displays the evolution of oven technology and creates an interesting twist in the spatial experience.

Alternating Use of Different Materials Adds Interest to the Space

Next to the red-brick structure, a fully-equipped classroom with movable doors and cooking stations provide a multi-functional area for try-out sessions and company events.

Passing windows with views to the exterior courtyard, one reaches the VIP lounge where exquisite dinners will be served. Lined with travertine stone slabs and walnut wood panels, this elegant room promises memorable gatherings. To top it all, guests are welcomed into the adjacent conservatory and outdoor courtyard where herbs are planted and picked to garnish their dishes.

Exhibition Space

Grupo Arca, Design Center Guadalajara

Design Agency
Esrawe Studio

Location
Guadalajara, Jalisco, Mexico

Area
5,701 m²

Photography
Genevieve Lutkin, Jaime Navarro, César Béjar

A quarry is the evidence of man's action on nature; a universe in which men unintentionally sculpt pleats and volumes that result in strange and visually striking geology. A manufactured landscape, an organic architecture created by the trace of the search for raw materials, which brings us back to the origin from which the raw materials come.

For the natural materials brand Grupo Arca, the architectural firm Esrawe Studio has designed a stone museum to showcase the raw materials and various stones sourced by the brand, presenting the chiselled, man-made landscape in the form of an organic building that returns to its roots.

Relaxed and Natural "Stone Forest"

The captivating and unique nature of this landscape nourishes the concept. The access through a small opening in the monolithic facade links the visitor with the central space of monumental character, the "arrival to the quarry", the Agora. The Agora is the starting point to begin a journey of museographic character, where the multiple exhibition halls with materials of diverse characteristics are articulated around, creating a dynamic and versatile experience.

The building is divided functionally and physically into two universes. Two separate volumes that are woven and related to each other: the universe of the quarry (which houses the Agora, the Design Center, the cafeteria, and the multipurpose room) and the warehouse, in which the experience ends. This warehouse acts and expresses itself as a container and distribution centre, a translucent and neutral space, a canvas that grants the relevance of the scene to the stones and that is framed in the background by a forest that links us again with the origin of matter.

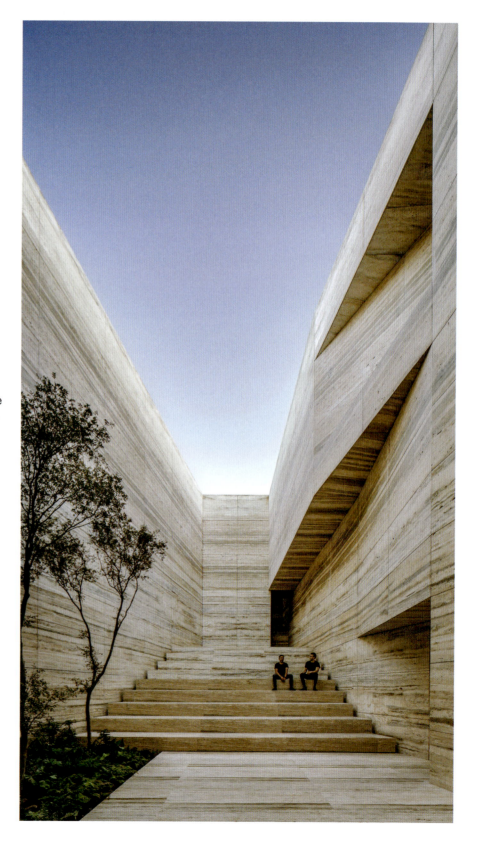

Making the Exhibition Hall a Vehicle for Cultural Transmission

The concept moves away from traditional retail space and promotes learning and dissemination, understanding of why and how architecture, design, art, and culture are generated in our country and worldwide. A platform that stimulates dialogue and knowledge; and establishes a relationship of mutual benefit with the community, its clients and partners; its main objective is to promote involvement in the construction of the cultural and creative expression of Mexico.

Technology plays a vital role because it allows the interaction of mobile devices with materials through QR codes. Thus, it immediately provides the user with the information, description, and costs of the selected materials, and allows the creation of a database of the contents of interest and the client's history, as well as analysing trends and purchasing behaviour.

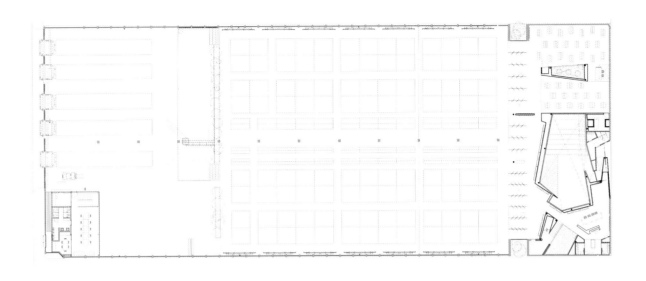
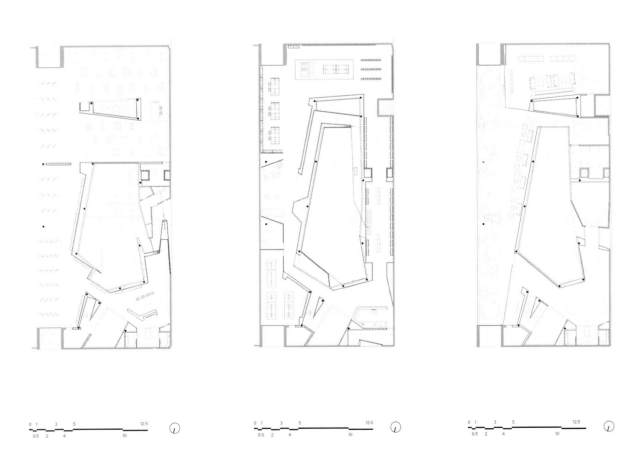

293

#

100architects
100architects.com
P164

A

ALA Architects
ala.fi
P052

ARTTA Concept Studio
www.arttaconceptstudio.com
P084

B

B+H Architects
bharchitects.com
P170

BIG-Bjarke Ingels Group
big.dk/#projects
P210

BLOCO Arquitetos
www.bloco.arq.br
P202

C

COORDINATION ASIA
www.coordination.asia
P242

D

Daipu Architects
www.daipuarchitects.com
P268

Department of ARCHITECTURE Co.
departmentofarchitecture.co.th
P040

E

Esrawe Studio
esrawe.com
P288

G

Guillaume Alan
www.guillaume-alan.com
P128

I

Ippolito Fleitz Group
ifgroup.org
P134

K

Klein Dytham Architecture
www.klein-dytham.com
P186

Kokaistudios
www.kokaistudios.com
P258

L

LUKSTUDIO
www.lukstudiodesign.com
P280

M

MAD Architect
www.i-mad.com
P028

MVRDV
www.mvrdv.nl
P022

N

Nendo
nendo.jp
P218

noa* (network of architecture)
www.noa.network
P064

O

Office of Architecture in Barcelona: OAB
ferrater.com
P250

OHLAB
ohlab.net
P094

P

Peny Hsieh Interiors
penyhsieh.com
P140

PES-Architects
www.pesark.com
P008

PLH Arkitekter A/S, Denmark
www.plh.dk
P178

S

Sevil Peach
www.sevilpeach.co.uk
P156

Studio Marco Piva
www.studiomarcopiva.com
P074

T

Teresa Sapey + Partners
www.teresasapey.com
P120

V

Vana Pernari Architecture Studio
www.vanapernari.com
P104

Vudafieri-Saverino Partners
www.vudafierisaverino.it
P226

W

Waterfrom Design
www.waterfrom.com
P194

Y

YOD Design Lab
yoddesign.com.ua
P236

Z

ZRIVERSTUDIO
zriverstudio.wixsite.com/zriver
P146

ARTPOWER

Acknowledgements

We would like to thank all the designers and companies who made significant contributions to the compilation of this book. Without them, this project would not have been possible. We would also like to thank many others whose names did not appear on the credits, but made specific input and support for the project from beginning to end.

Future Editions

If you would like to contribute to the next edition of Artpower, please email us your details to: press@artpower.com.cn